Best Inspir

1000 Positive Quotes to Motivate and Inspire You

Jason James

PUBLISHED BY:
Jason James
Copyright © 2013

All rights reserved.

No part of this publication may be copied, reproduced in any format, by any means, electronic or otherwise, without prior consent from the copyright owner and publisher of this book.

Disclaimer

The information contained in this book is for general information purposes only. The information is provided by the authors and while we endeavor to keep the information up to date and correct, we make no representations or warranties of any kind, express or implied, about the completeness, accuracy, reliability, suitability or availability with respect to the book or the information, products, services, or related graphics contained in the book for any purpose. Any reliance you place on such information is therefore strictly at your own risk.

Benson Kua/flickr
http://www.flickr.com/photos/bensonkua/3112828024/sizes/o/in/photolist-

1. "It is a fine thing to have ability, but the ability to discover ability in others is the true test." — Elbert Hubbard

2. "A man with ability and the desire to accomplish something can do anything." - Donald Kircher

3. "He is able who thinks he is able." — Buddha

4. "Great ability develops and reveals itself increasingly with every new assignment." - Baltasar Gracian, The Oracle

5. "A person who aims at nothing is sure to hit it." — Anon

6. "We are told never to cross a bridge until we come to it, but this world is owned by men who have 'crossed bridges' in their imagination far ahead of the crowd." — Anon

7. "No bird soars too high if he soars with his own wings." - William Blake

8. "Shoot for the moon. Even if you miss, you'll land among the stars." - Les Brown

9. "You can't build a reputation on what you're going to do." - Henry Ford

10. "To accomplish great things, we must not only act, but also dream; not only plan, but also believe " - Anatole France

11. "The best way out is always through." - Robert Frost

12. "The entrepreneur is essentially a visualizer and an actualizer... He can visualize something, and when he visualizes it he sees exactly how to make it happen." - Robert L. Schwartz

13. "The roots of true achievement lie in the will to become the best that you can become." - Harold Taylor

14. "Keep away from people who try to belittle your ambitions. Small people always do that, but the really great make you feel that you, too, can become great." - Mark Twain

15. "If you can imagine it you can achieve it. If you can dream it, you can become it." - William Arthur Ward

Andy Wright/ flickr
http://www.flickr.com/photos/95172615@N00/224639076/in/photolist-

16. "The tears that you spill, the sorrowful, are sweeter than the laughter of snobs and the guffaws of scoffers." - Kahlil Gibran

17. "No pessimist ever discovered the secret of the stars, or sailed to an uncharted land, or opened a new doorway for the human spirit." - Helen Keller

18. "A will finds a way." - Orison Swett Marden

19. "Every exit is an entry somewhere." - Tom Stoppard

20. "The cynic knows the price of everything and the value of nothing." - Oscar Wilde

21. "You can complain because roses have thorns, or you can rejoice because thorns have roses." – Ziggy

22. "Attitude produces character, and character produces hope." - Mark Brunett

23. "Character is the real foundation for all worthwhile success" - John Hays Hammond

24. "Character is power. It makes friends, draws patronage and support, and opens a sure way to wealth, honor, and happiness." - John Howe

25. "Personality can open doors, but only character can keep them open." - Elmer G. Letterman

26. "Our character is what we do when we think no one is looking." - H. Jackson Brown, Jr.

27. "To measure the man, measure his heart." - Malcolm Stevenson Forbes

28. "The true test of character is not how much we know how to do, but how we behave when we don't know what to do." - John Holt

29. "Many a man's reputation would not know his character if they met on the street." - Elbert Hubbard

30. "Character cannot be developed in ease and quiet. Only through experience of trial and suffering can the soul be strengthened, ambition inspired, and success achieved." - Helen Keller

31. "A loving person lives in a loving world. A hostile person lives in a hostile world. Everyone you meet is your mirror." - Ken Keys

32. "The ultimate measure of a man is not where he stands in moments of comfort, but where he stands at times of challenge and controversy." - Martin Luther King, Jr.

33. "Nearly all men can stand adversity, but if you want to test a man's character, give him power." - Abraham Lincoln

34. "Bluntness is a virtue." - Allison Ling

35. "The measure of a man's real character is what he would do if he knew he would never be found out." - Thomas B. Macaulay

36. "When you choose your friends, don't be short-changed by choosing personality over character." - W. Somerset Maugham

37. "If you don't know where you're going, you'll end up somewhere else" - Yogi Berra

38. "Our aspirations are our possibilities" - Robert Browning

39. "Concentrate on finding your goal, then concentrate on reaching it." - Col. Michael Friedsam

40. "The journey of a thousand miles begins with one step." - Lao-Tzu

41. "Determine that the thing can and shall be done, and then we shall find a way." - Abraham Lincoln

42. "Shoot for the moon, even if you miss, you'll land among the stars." - Les Brown

43. "Our goals can only be reached through a vehicle of a plan, in which we must fervently believe, and upon which we must vigorously act. There is no other route to success." - Stephen A. Brennan

44. "Obstacles are those frightful things you see when you take your eyes off your goal." - Henry Ford

45. "This one step -- choosing a goal and sticking to it -- changes everything." - Scott Reed

46. "The indispensable first step to getting the things you want out of life is this: decide what you want." - Ben Stein

47. "Honesty is the cornerstone of character." - B.C. Forbes

48. "Honesty is the first chapter in the book of wisdom." - Thomas Jefferson

49. "No legacy is so rich as honesty." - William Shakespeare

50. "Each time you are honest and conduct yourself with honesty, a success force will drive you toward greater success. Each time you lie, even with a little white lie, there are strong forces pushing you toward failure." - Joseph Sugarman

51. "Great hopes make great men." - Thomas Fuller

52. "Hope is a waking dream." – Aristotle

Katie Boord/flickr

http://www.flickr.com/photos/78658559@N06/8315831432/in/photolist-

53. "The men who build the future are those who know that greater things are yet to come, and that they themselves will help bring them about. Their minds are illuminated by the blazing sun of home. They never stop to doubt. They haven't time." - Melvin J. Evans

54. "There is no medicine like hope, no incentive so great, no tonic so powerful as expectation of something tomorrow." - Orison S. Marden

55. "Of all the forces that make for a better world, none is so indispensable, none so powerful, as hope. Without hope men are only half alive. With hope they dream and think and work." - Charles Sawyer

56. "Aerodynamically, the bumble bee shouldn't be able to fly, but the bumble bee doesn't know it so it goes on flying anyway.' - Mary Kay Ash

57. "Most of the important things in the world have been accomplished by people who have kept on trying when there seemed to be no hope at all." - Dale Carnegie

58. "If you have a lemon, make lemonade." - Howard Gossage

59. "Hope is a state of mind, not of the world. Hope, in this deep and powerful sense, is not the same as joy that things are going well, or willingness to invest in enterprises that are obviously heading for success, but rather an ability to work for something because it is good." - Vaclav Havel

60. "A leader is one who knows the way, shows the way, and goes the way." - Author Unknown

61. "A leader is a dealer of hope." - Napoleon Bonaparte

62. "Real leaders are ordinary people, with extraordinary determinations" - John Seaman Garns

63. "Leadership is an action, not a position." - Donald H. McGannon

64. "A great leader never sets himself above his followers except in carrying responsibilities." - Jules Ormont

65. "A real leader faces the music, even when he doesn't like the tune." - Anon

66. "Good leaders make people feel that they're at the very heart of things, not at the periphery. Everyone feels that he or she makes a difference to the success of the organization. When that happens people feel centered and that gives their work meaning." - Warren Bennis

67. "I am certainly not one of those who need to be prodded. In fact, if anything, I am the prod." - Sir Winston Churchill

68. "Effective leadership is putting first things first. Effective management is discipline, carrying it out." - Stephen Covey

69. "The first responsibility of a leader is to define reality. The last is to say thank you. In between, the leader is a servant." - Max De Pree

70. "Leadership is the art of getting someone else to do something you want done because he wants to do it." - Dwight D. Eisenhower

71. "In simplest terms, a leader is one who knows where he wants to go, and gets up, and goes." - John Erksine

72. "One of the tests of leadership is the ability to recognize a problem before it becomes an emergency." - John Glassgow

73. "The very essence of leadership is that you have to have a vision." - Theodore Hesburgh

74. "The difference between a boss and a leader: a boss says, 'Go!' - a leader says, 'Let's go!'" - E.M. Kelly

75. "The leader who exercises power with honor will work from the inside out, starting with himself." - Blaine Lee

76. "The great leaders are like the best conductors - they reach beyond the notes to reach the magic in the players." - Blaine Lee

77. "The final test of a leader is that he leaves behind him in other men the conviction and the will to carry on." - Walter Lippmann

78. "The genius of a good leader is to leave behind him a situation which common sense, without the grace of genius, can deal with successfully." - Walter Lippman

79. "To command is to serve, nothing more and nothing less." - Andre Malraux, Man's Hope

80. "The ultimate leader is one who is willing to develop people to the point that they eventually surpass him or her in knowledge and ability." - Fred A. Manske, Jr.

81. "Leadership is a combination of strategy and character. If you must be without one, be without the strategy." - Gen. H. Norman Schwarzkopf

82. "No amount of study or learning will make a man a leader unless he has the natural qualities of one." - Archibald Wavell

83. "A wise man will make more opportunities than he finds." - Francis Bacon

84. "The way to miss success is to miss the opportunity." - Victor Chasles

85. "We are confronted with insurmountable opportunities." - Walt Kelly

86. "Opportunity has power over all things." - Sophocles

87. "An optimist sees an opportunity in every calamity, a pessimist sees a calamity in every opportunity." - Sir Winston Churchill

Lucas/flickr
http://www.flickr.com/photos/22558336@N06/2372487324/in/photolist-

88. "If it exists, it's possible." - John P. Grier

89. "Opportunities are usually disguised as hard work, so most people don't recognize them." - Ann Landers

90. "The golden opportunity you are seeking is in yourself. It is not in your environment; it is not in luck or chance, or the help of others; it is in yourself alone." - Orison Swett Marden

91. "Most successful men have not achieved their distinction by having some new talent or opportunity presented to them. They have developed the opportunity that was at hand." - Bruce Marten

92. "We are confronted with insurmountable opportunities." - Pogo

93. "The doors we open and close each day decide the lives we live." - Flora Whittemore

94. "Whatever strengthens and purifies the affections, enlarges the imagination, and adds spirit to sense, is useful." - Percy Bysshe Shelley

95. "Greatness lies not in being strong, but in the right using of strength." - Henry Ward Beecher

96. "I learned that it is the weak who are cruel, and that gentleness is to be expected only from the strong." - Leo Rosten

97. "We deceive ourselves when we fancy that only weakness needs support. Strength needs it far more." - Madame Swetchine, The Writings of Madame Swetchine

98. "Success requires the vision to see, the faith to believe, and the courage to do." - Author Unknown

99. "Ambition, confidence, enthusiasm and success are produced by courage, faith, pride, and hard work." - Harry F. Banks

100. "Success is not a matter of desire, but the product of hard work." - Jack Barringer

101. "To succeed, one must possess an effective combination of ability, ambition, courage, drive, hard work, integrity, and loyalty." - Harry F. Banks

102. "Never mind what others do; better than yourself, beat your own record from day to do, and you are a success." - William J.H. Boetckner

103. "If you find it in your heart to care for somebody else, you will have succeeded." - Maya Angelou

104. "They never fail who die in a great cause." - George Gordon Byron

105. "The important thing to recognize is that it takes a team, and the team ought to get credit for the wins and the losses. Successes have many fathers, failures have none." - Philip Caldwell

106. "I don't know the key to success, but the key to failure is to try to please everyone." - Bill Cosby

107. "To laugh often and much; to win the respect of intelligent people and the affection of children; to earn the appreciation of honest critics and endure the betrayal of false friends; to appreciate beauty, to find the best in others; to leave the world a little better; whether by a healthy child, a garden patch or a redeemed social condition; to know even one life has breathed easier because you have lived. This is the meaning of success." - Ralph Waldo Emerson

108. "The majority of men meet with failure because of their lack of persistence in creating new plans to take the place of those which fail." - Napoleon Hill

109. "Only those who dare to fail greatly can ever achieve greatly." - Robert Francis Kennedy

110. "It's not failure, but low aim is crime." – Lowell

111. "Success is that old ABC -- ability, breaks, and courage." - Charles Luckman

112. "You may be disappointed if you fail, but you are doomed if you don't try." - Beverly Sills

113. "The only time you don't fail is the last time you try anything -- and it works." - William Strong

114. "Men are born to succeed, not to fail." - Henry David Thoreau

115. "Defeat is not the worst of failures. Not to have tried is the true failure." - George E. Woodberry

116. "Walk into darkness to relight the candle that has burnt out in someone else's world... then, you will learn the true meaning of life." - Angula R. Fuhr

117. "You never know when you will meet an amazing person and when you do, let them know just how amazing they are." -Renee Scalfni

118. "Rise above the unpleasant times as much as you can and savor the good ones." - Rita DeCelles

119. "In difficult times we are often overwhelmed with worry. But remember, contentment comes not through having, but through knowing that God will supply all our needs." -Shane Smith

120. "Already, God in good measure sends angels to you - to watch over and protect too and give you comfort anew and encouragement in heavenly dew. Be blessed and remain sanctified with goodness." - Hercolena Oliver

121. "Though I'm imperfect, I realize, GOD made me perfect, just uniquely perfect... to exist in an imperfect world, just perfectly." - Marion Stokes

122. "I am one with the Power that created me. I am totally open and receptive to the abundant flow of prosperity that the Universe offers. All my needs and desires are met before I even ask. I am Divinely guided and protected, and I make choices that are beneficial for me. I rejoice in other's successes, knowing there is plenty for us all." - Louise Hay

123. "If you would create something, you must be something." - Johann Wolfgang von Goethe

124. "Rejoice in the things that are present; all else is beyond thee." - Michel de Montaigne

125. "I live my life in widening rings which spread over earth and sky. I may not ever complete the last one, but that is what l will try. I circle around God's primordial tower, and l circle ten thousand years long; And l still don't know if I'm a falcon, a storm, or a unfinished song." - Rainer Marie Rilke

126. "HOPE & END" are always there for everybody - it depends on us how we deal with them - "A HOPELESS END" or "AN ENDLESS HOPE"." - Author Unknown

127. "However many blessings we expect from God, His infinite liberality will always exceed all our wishes and our thoughts." - Author Unknown

128. "There are certain things that drive my life: emotion, vision, passion, compassion and inspiration. These things reside inside my spirit (heart) and are transferred into my mind, from my mind to my body and my body transforms it into action." - Sheye Hassan

129. "A day will come when we'll be rewarded for making mistakes earlier in our lives because we get better with each one of them

and do things the right way when they are more important!" - Ravi Kant

130. "Love is the one option that is always open to you. Love awakens and enhances all of our senses. Love makes you feel overwhelmed with joy. Speak kind words and you will hear kind echoes. The measure of our poverty or of our wealth is the love we give to others. Appreciation makes people feel more important than almost anything else in the world. When there is love in the heart, it just naturally spreads to others. The world needs more warm and loving hearts. I wish everyone days with Joy, Peaceful nights and life full of LOVE." - Marita Manalo Domingo

131. "The wise man in the storm prays to God, not for safety from danger, but deliverance from fear." - Author Unknown

Zdenko Zivkovic/flickr
http://www.flickr.com/photos/zivkovic/6040888856/

132. "I want peace. Drop 'I' for it denotes ego and drop 'want' for it indicates desire. Peace shall be yours." - Author Unknown

133. "The quote is in tune with Hindu scriptures, which advocates curbing of ego and desires. While ego breeds arrogance, unfulfilled desires cause anger, loss of wisdom leading to complete ruin. Peace is attained by negating self and accepting God's love and grace. Just when you think you can't get through something. . . you blink and God's like, 'Hello, you just did!'" - Maria Martinez

134. "Each day will pass but as darkness sets in, rejoice. Give thanks that you survived the day that was, with all its good and bad. And as you arise tomorrow, let the rising sun be a reflection of your hope - renewed & always present; of your spirit - shining, even through the clouds. And let those with whom you come in contact feel your ever warming presence. SHINE!" - Shane Smith

135. "We are all born with music in our hearts. Some choose to let it be heard." - Thomas P. Fouts

136. "When we were creating the Blue Star Music Camp, a week-long summer camp to teach kids music, dance, and song, I came up with that saying/quote. We made a poster out of it and displayed it in the lobby of the camp. It came to me in a dream one night after an inspiring night of work. I quickly wrote it down and that is how it came about. There are only two things we can do in our life: dream and to make our dreams come true." - Vaiga L

137. "I came up with this quote when I felt like I was stuck in one place without the possibility to move or to do anything meaningful at my life - like my days were going nowhere, though I had thousands of dreams and goals to reach. And then I understood that there are times when there is nothing you can possibly do, nothing you even have to do; that there are times just to dream, to relax and to wait. And after that, if you stay focused, the times to act certainly will come; the times and possibilities to make these dreams come true. There are many persons ready to do what is right because in their heart they know it is right. But, they hesitate, waiting for the other fellow to make the first move - and he, in turn, waits for you. The minute a person dares to take the open-hearted and courageous way, many others follow." - Marian Anderson

138. "On the mural of life, I'm God's work of art. So are you. . . He keeps painting us till we become masterpieces. We keep unfolding." - Stanley Anukege

139. "To wake up in the morning is just more than waking! It's another day to be thankful for, another day to have a job, to have family, friends, complaints and obstacles that life puts us through. Another day isn't promised so treat life as a special occasion everyday! Love, Laugh, Learn for no reason at all! I know I do!" – Author Unknown

140. "You have succeeded in life when all you really want is only what you really need." - Vernon Howard

141. "I selected this one because success comes only from burning desire and burning desire comes only from necessity. Necessity is the mother of invention and root of all success" – Author Unknown

142. "To live your life with Love for all living things is a great time spent and will outlast forever and beyond another." - Marita Manalo Domingo

143. "Be like a flute, let him play your life's song freely; don't interrupt him with your ego, let him take over all you have." - Author Unknown

144. "Our faith must be alive. It cannot be just a set of rigid beliefs and notions. Our faith must evolve every day and bring us joy, peace, freedom and love." - Thich Nhat Hanh

145. "Nothing is stronger than love." - Author Unknown

146. "A meteorite looks beautiful but stays in sight for a few seconds while a star looks beautiful and stays in sight for life." - Vibhore Jain

147. "When the weight of the world becomes your problem, you need to trust in God and leave it all in his hands and he will see

you through. Until then, chill out and let God have his way." - Author Unknown

148. "There never was a great soul that did not have some divine inspiration." – Cicero

149. "The most spiritual human beings, assuming they are the most courageous, also experience by far the most painful tragedies: but it is precisely for this reason that they honor life, because it brings against them its most formidable weapons." - Friedrich Nietzsche

150. "The soul loves to meditate, for in contact with the Spirit lies its greatest joy. If, then you experience mental resistance during meditation, remember that reluctance to meditate comes from the ego; it doesn't belong to the soul." - Paramahansa Yogananda

151. "It is better to have a cancer of the body than of the mind, heart, or Spirit." - Debra Anne Keay

152. "When I try hard, don't succeed and see only darkness; when I have no hope and decide to give it up, God shows omens of his existence and gives me the best I deserve." - Pradnya Potdar

153. "No matter how old you are, love and embrace how young you feel and know it truly helps you deal with all the trials and tribulations of these crazy nations. Keep your head up high, the Lord's strength will get you by!" - Jessica Urban

154. "Unite to move forward." - American Proverb

155. "Progress is the activity of today and the assurance of tomorrow." - Ralph Waldo Emerson

156. "Fundamental progress has to do with the reinterpretation of basic ideas." - Alfred North Whitehead

157. "Plan your progress carefully; hour-by hour, day-by-day, month-by-month.

Organized activity and maintained enthusiasm are the wellsprings of your power." - Paul J. Meyer

158. "If there is no struggle, there is no progress." - Frederick Douglass

159. "People fascinated by the idea of progress never suspect that every step forward is also a step on the way to the end." - Milan Kundera

160. "Change does not necessarily assure progress, but progress implacably requires change. Education is essential to change, for education creates both new wants and the ability to satisfy them." - Henry Steele Commager

161. "If I were required to guess off-hand, and without collusion with higher minds, what is the bottom cause of the amazing material and intellectual advancement of the last fifty years, I should guess that it was the modern-born and previously non-existent disposition on the part of men to believe that a new idea can have value." - Mark Twain

162. "Discontent is the first step in the progress of a man or a nation." - Oscar Wilde

163. "The chief obstacle to the progress of the human race is the human race." - Don Marquis

164. "All progress is based upon a universal innate desire on the part of every organism to live beyond its income." - Samuel Butler

165. "Respect the past in the full measure of its desserts, but do not make the mistake of confusing it with the present nor seek in it the ideals of the future." - Jose Incenerios

166. "Life can only be understood backwards; but it must be lived forwards."- Soren Kierkegaard

167. "Never discourage anyone...who continually makes progress, no matter how slow."– Plato

168. "Optimism is essential to achievement and it is also the foundation of courage and true progress." - Nicholas Murray Butler

169. "All progress occurs because people dare to be different." - Harry Milner

170. "True progress quietly and persistently moves along without notice." - St. Francis of Assisi

171. "Don't shoot for something unattainable – completely outside of your nature or opportunity." - Michael Johnson

172. "Always bear in mind that your own resolution to succeed is more important than any one thing." - Abraham Lincoln

173. "It is possible to fail in many ways…while to succeed is possible only in one way." – Aristotle

174. "Man is not made for defeat. A man can be destroyed, but not defeated." - Ernest Hemingway

175. "You learn as much from those who have failed as from those who have succeeded." - Michael Johnson

176. "The road to success is lined with many tempting parking spaces." - Traditional Proverb

177. "If your success is not on your own terms, if it looks good to the world but does not feel good in your heart, it is not success at all." - Anna Quindlen

178. "It's nice to be the best, but not when being the best brings out the worst in you." - Rodney Dangerfield

179. "You can make goals for family, relationships, anything." - Michael Johnson

180. "To succeed, you need to take that gut feeling in what you believe and act on it with all of your heart."   - Christy Borgeld

181. "Real success is finding your lifework in the work that you love." - David McCullough

182. "Success is counted sweetest by those who ne'er succeed." - Emily Dickinson

183. "I owe my success to having listened respectfully to the very best advice, and then going away and doing the exact opposite." - G. K. Chesterton

184. "You owe it to yourself to find your own unorthodox way of succeeding, or sometimes, just surviving."- Michael Johnson

185. "To freely bloom - that is my definition of success."- Gerry Spence

186. "Success usually comes to those who are too busy to be looking for it." - Henry David Thoreau

187. "People rarely succeed unless they have fun in what they are doing" - Dale Carnegie

188. "From success to failure is one step; from failure to success is a long road." - Yiddish Proverb

189. "Try not to become a man of success but rather to become a man of value." - Albert Einstein

190. "(Natural Talent + Opportunity) Hard Work = Success."- Michael Johnson

191. "There are defeats more triumphant than victories." - Michel Montaigne

192. "It is clearly not the journey for everyone. People succeed in as many ways as there are people. Some can be completely fulfilled with destinations that are much closer to home and more comfortable. But if you long to keep going, then I hope you are able to follow my lead to the places I have gone. To within a whisper of your own personal perfection. To places that are

sweeter because you worked so hard to arrive there. To places at the very edge of your dreams." - Michael Johnson

193. "Each time someone stands up for an ideal, or acts to improve the lot of others, or strikes out against injustice, he sends forth a tiny ripple of hope." - Robert F. Kennedy

194. "Every time we open our mouths, men look into our minds." – Anonymous

195. "Everyone's life is an object lesson to others." - Karl G. Maeser

196. "Example sheds a genial ray which men are apt to borrow, so first improve yourself today, and then your friends tomorrow." –Anonymous

197. "You really can change the world if you care enough." - Marion Wright Edelman

198. "The reasonable man adapts himself to the world. The unreasonable man adapts the world to himself. All progress depends upon the unreasonable man." - George Bernard Shaw

199. "Tell me and I forget; show me and I remember; involve me and I understand." – Anonymous

200. "I'd rather see a sermon than hear one any day; I'd rather have one walk beside me than merely point the way." - David O. McKay

201. "A gentle hand may lead even an elephant by a single hair." - Iranian Proverb

202. "The pessimist complains about the wind. The optimist expects it to change. The leader adjusts the sails." - John Maxwell

203. "The function of leadership is to produce more leaders, not more followers." - Ralph Nader

204. "Let's not just transform those in need, we can also find ways to help transform those in power." – Anonymous

205. "One machine can do the work of fifty ordinary men. No machine can do the work of one extraordinary man." - Elbert Hubbard

206. "The best leader brings out the best in those he has stewardship over." - J. Richard Clarke

207. "Nearly all men can stand adversity, but if you want to test a man's character, give him power." –Anonymous

208. "The greatest good you can do for another is not just share your riches, but reveal to them their own." - Benjamin Disraeli

209. "Don't call me a saint - I don't want to be dismissed that easily." - Dorothy Day

210. "Let your light shine before men, that they may see your good deeds and praise your Father in heaven." - Matthew 5:15 (see also v.14- 16)

211. "The test we must set for ourselves is not to march alone but to march in such a way that others will wish to join us." - Hubert Humphrey, U.S. vice president, senator

212. "He that would be a leader must be a bridge." - Welsh Proverb

213. "The best leaders of all, the people know not they exist. They turn to each other and say, We did it ourselves."- Zen Proverb

214. "It is our choices...that show what we truly are, far more than our abilities." - J. K. Rowling

215. "We have no simple problems or easy decisions after kindergarten." - John W. Turk

216. "Again and again, the impossible problem is solved when we see that the problem is only a tough decision waiting to be made." - Robert H. Schuller

217. "Who moves picks up, who stands still, dries up" -.Italian Proverb.

218. "The journey of a thousand miles begins with a single step." -Lao Tzu

219. "Industry is the parent of success." - Spanish Proverb

220. "Thought is the seed of action." - Ralph Waldo Emerson

221. "What lies behind us and what lies before us are tiny matters compared to what lies within us." - Ralph Waldo Emerson

222. "Self-trust is the first secret of success." - Ralph Waldo Emerson

223. "When it is dark enough, you can see the stars." - Persian Proverb

224. "You must know for which harbor you are headed if you are to catch the right wind to take you there." – Seneca

225. "Lots of things that couldn't be done have been done." - Charles Auston Bates

226. "The winds and the waves are always on the side of the ablest navigators." - Edward Gibbon

227. "They can conquer who believe they can." - Ralph Waldo Emerson

228. "There are glimpses of heaven to us in every act, or thought, or word, that raises us above ourselves." - A. P. Stanley

229. "Be not afraid of greatness: some are born great, some achieve greatness, and some have greatness thrust upon them." - William Shakespeare

230. "People who ask confidently get more than those who are hesitant and uncertain. When you've figured out what you want to ask for, do it with certainty, boldness and confidence." - Jack Canfield

231. "The weak are blind; champions visualize their dreams and goals and stop at nothing to see them as a reality." - Samy

232. " Positive thinking is nothing unless you take a positive action. An action is nothing unless you face challenges and rejections. Think positively, plan creatively and act differently is the way of success." - Ramesh Thapa

233. " Time tests everyone; many of us crumble. But the brave ones stand, fight and get honors." - Mehul Grover

234. "Don't tell me the problem is tough. If it is not tough, then it is not a problem." - Author Unknown

235. " There is always a solution for every problem; you only need to put your efforts in the right direction." - Rakesh Bagri

Robert Fornal/flickr
http://www.flickr.com/photos/64251830@N00/364312031/in/photolist-

236. " You've tried then failed. You've tried again then failed again. Don't give up. TRY it again; you're almost there." - Johni Pangalila

237. "There is no stimulus like that which comes from the consciousness of knowing that others believe in us." - Orison Swett Marden

238. "Greatness will never manifest until it's first perceived then released by the one who holds it." - Yolanda F. Presley

239. " I have not failed. It's just that the distance between me and my destiny has increased and I have gained some experience." - Zoya Khan

240. " Achievement is directly proportional to enthusiasm." - Pramod Kumar Sharma

241. "Look around. What do you see that is good? Savor it!" - Pam Malafronte

242. "Today was yesterday's battle; tomorrow is today's dream." - Roxanne Hoffner

243. "I am the best and I love being the best, always, because being the best gets you to the best." - Jiten Soni

244. "It's when we stop forcing it ... trying to impress... that we really shine through. We start having strong people, like us, just fall into our laps and those that are weak are empowered by the tone of our voice." - Miles Patrick Yohnke

245. "If you're honest, dedicated and committed, no one can pull you down." - Shaheem Mahir

246. "We run from failure... we run from success... but what really matters is not what we're running from, but where we are running to!" - M. Goerz

247. "Success is my shadow." - Varun Arora

248. "No one in the world was ever you before, with your particular gifts and abilities and possibilities. It's a shame to waste those by doing what someone else has done." - Joseph Campbell

249. "If I claim to love my job, then arguing about what I should take from it is out of the question. Giving and taking is when you do a transaction. When it comes to do the job you love, giving is what it's all about!" - Hingdranata Nikolay

250. "A man is known by the company he keeps." - Author Unknown

251. "The World will begin to be right in my eyes when warships are filled with food and that food is distributed families in need." - Jesse Barkasy

252. "Experience is a Teacher that teaches you how to fight during failure and how to conquer success." - Dr. Pravin Dhikale

253. "What you give your time to - is what you will own or have." - T.N

254. "What is the most important thing? Anything on the left side of the equal sign. That's what you're really working on." - Ikhwan Sopa

255. "Fight your situation, without hesitation, because you have a revelation that will lead you to your destination." - Author Unknown

256. "There is no reward for doing what's right. Doing what's right should not be an option but should be a priority. So become selfish to yourself until you achieve your goals." - Author Unknown

257. "So long as there is a Bagpiper to play the Great War Pipes, shall our nation remain Scotland the Brave, Scotland the Free!" - King Robert the Bruce

258. "I cannot give you the formula for success, but I can give you the formula for failure--which is:
Try to please everybody." - Herbert Bayard Swope

259. "The difference between a successful person and others is not a lack of strength, not a lack of knowledge, but rather a lack in will." - Vince Lombardi

260. "Companies don't create winners, but winners create companies." - Gigs Gasper

261. "People get hired for their skills and fired for their attitudes." - Author Unknown

262. "Success and excuses don't work together and the most important thing in success - is learning to overcome failure." - Tomiwa Akinsegun

263. "To be able to lead others, a man must be willing to go forward alone." - Author Unknown

264. "Success introduces you to the world while defeat introduces the world to you." - Author Unknown

265. "Those who really want to succeed must give up, once and for all, 'nibbling' at things. Take up one idea, make that idea your life; think of it, live on that idea. Let the brain, muscles, nerves, every part of your body, be full of that idea and just leave every other ideas alone. This is the way to success." - Swami Vivekananda

266. "Problems can only be solved by action, not by contemplation. But all great minds like yours must think thoroughly before they act. So when challenges come your way, as they inevitably will, think, pray, listen, then act." - Shane Smith

267. "Consistency is a key to success. To keep it with you, always keep trying." - Dr.Pravin Dhikale

268. "Be humble but be confident in your abilities." - Robert Moore

269. "Always, always, be happy doing what you are doing. If you are not happy, no matter how well you do it, leave it. It truly is all about the happy part." - Tammie L. Judy

270. "If you enter this world knowing you are loved and you leave this world knowing the same, then everything that happens in between can be dealt with." - Michael Jackson

gf97127272/flickr
http://www.flickr.com/photos/short-bus-rider/3323528303/

271. "Failures do what is tension relieving, while winners do what is goal achieving." - Dennis Waitley

272. "Do not despise your days of small beginnings; they will add up one day." - Anthony Thuo

273. "The greatest results in life are usually attained by simple means and the exercise of ordinary qualities. These may for the most part be summed in these two: common-sense and **perseverance**." - Owen Feltham

274. "Everyday we look and strive for greater things and if we just looked in the mirror... We would find "Greatness"." - Cathy Choi

275. "Dreams are only potential actions that exist in the heart of the faithful." - Tara Tull

276. "Blessed is the person who sees the need, recognizes the responsibility, and actively becomes the answer." - William Ward

277. "We are all inventors, each sailing out on a voyage of discovery, guided each by a private chart, of which there is no duplicate. The world is all gates, all opportunities." - Ralph Waldo Emerson

278. "Seek the lofty by reading, hearing and seeing great work at some moment every day." - Thornton Wilder

279. "The only way of finding the limits of the possible is by going beyond them into the impossible." - Arthur C. Clarke

280. "Without inspiration the best powers of the mind remain dormant. There is a fuel in us which needs to be ignited with sparks." - Johann Gottfried Von Herder

281. "We are what we repeatedly do. Excellence, therefore, is not an act but a habit." – Aristotle

282. "Work spares us from three evils: boredom, vice, and need." – Voltaire

283. "Experience is the child of thought, and thought is the child of action." - Benjamin Disraeli

284. "You cannot plough a field by turning it over in your mind." - Author Unknown

285. "The best way out is always through." - Robert Frost

286. "Do not wait to strike till the iron is hot; but make it hot by striking." - William B. Sprague

287. "Nothing will ever be attempted if all possible objections must first be overcome." - Samuel Johnson

288. "Fortune favors the brave." - Publius Terence

289. "When the best things are not possible, the best may be made of those that are." - Richard Hooker

290. "He who hesitates is lost." -Unknown Author

291. "Great spirits have always encountered violent opposition from mediocre minds."- Albert Einstein

292. "Knowing is not enough; we must apply. Willing is not enough; we must do." - Johann Wolfgang von Goethe

293. "We are still masters of our fate. We are still captains of our souls." - Winston Churchill

294. "Nothing great was ever achieved without enthusiasm." - Ralph Waldo Emerson

295. "For hope is but the dream of those that wake." - Matthew Prior

296. "Constant dripping hollows out a stone." – Lucretius

297. "Nothing contributes so much to tranquilize the mind as a steady purpose-- a point on which the soul may fix its intellectual eye." - Mary Shelley

298. "Along with success comes a reputation for wisdom." – Euripides

299. "They can because they think they can." – Virgil

300. "Nothing can stop the man with the right mental attitude from achieving his goal; nothing on earth can help the man with the wrong mental attitude. " - Thomas Jefferson

301. "Keep steadily before you the fact that all true success depends at last upon yourself." - Theodore T. Hunger

302. "We are all motivated by a keen desire for praise, and the better a man is, the more he is inspired to glory." – Cicero

303. "Success is the sum of small efforts, repeated day in and day out." - Robert Collier

304. "The thing always happens that you really believe in; and the belief in a thing makes it happen." - Frank Loyd Wright

305. "A failure is a man who has blundered, but is not able to cash in on the experience." - Elbert Hubbard

306. "There is only one success--to be able to spend your life in your own way." - Christopher Morley

307. "Success is sweet: the sweeter if long delayed and attained through manifold struggles and defeats." - A. Branson Alcott

308. "The secret of success is to know something nobody else knows." - Aristotle Onassis

309. "Failures do what is tension relieving, while winners do what is goal achieving." - Dennis Waitley

310. "The difference between a successful person and others is not a lack of strength, not a lack of knowledge, but rather a lack in will." - Vince Lombardi

311. "I cannot give you the formula for success, but I can give you the formula for failure--which is:
Try to please everybody." - Herbert Bayard Swope

312. "Success does not consist in never making blunders, but in never making the same one a second time." - Josh Billings

313. "The secret of success in life is for a man to be ready for his opportunity when it comes." - Earl of Beaconsfield

314. "Success is the good fortune that comes from aspiration, desperation, perspiration and inspiration." - Evan Esar

315. "The surest way not to fail is to determine to succeed." - Richard Brinsley Sheridan

316. "If you wish success in life, make perseverance your bosom friend, experience your wise counselor, caution your elder brother, and hope your guardian genius." - Jospeph Addison

317. "Impatience never commanded success." - Edwin H. Chapin

318. "Courage is not the absence of fear, but rather the judgment that something else is more important than fear. " - Author Unknown

319. "You've got to follow your passion. You've got to figure out what it is you love--who you really are. And have the courage to do that. I believe that the only courage anybody ever needs is the courage to follow your own dreams." - Oprah Winfrey

320. "Obstacles are those frightful things when you take your eyes of your goal" - Henry Ford

321. "Obstacles are put in our way to see if what we want is really worth fighting for." -Author Unknown

322. "Only as high as I reach can I grow only as far as I seek can I go, Only as deep as I look can I see, only as much as I dream can I be." -Kare Ravn

323. "He is a wise man who does not grieve for the things which he has not, but rejoices for those which he has." -Epictetus

324. "You must be the change you wish to see in the world." -Gandhi

325. "Nothing will ever be attempted if all possible objections must first be overcome." -Samuel Johnson

326. "Limitations live only in our minds. But if we use our imaginations, our possibilities become limitless." -Jamie Paolinetti

327. "Life is not measured by the number of breaths we take, but by the moments that take our breath away."   -George Carlin

328. "No one can make you feel inferior without your consent." -Eleanor Roosevelt

329. "Twenty years from now you will be more disappointed by the things you didn't do thank by the ones you did do. SO throw off the bowlines. Sail away from the safe harbor. Catch the trade winds in your sails. Explore. Dream." -Mark Twain

330. "Two roads diverged in a wood, and I … I took the one less traveled by and that has made all the difference." -Robert Frost

331. "What lies behind us and what lies before us are tiny matters compared to what lies within us."   -Ralph Waldo Emerson

332. "The only thing we have to fear is fear itself" -Franklin D. Roosevelt

333. "Destiny is not a matter of chance, It is a matter of choice. It is not something to be waited for, But rather something to be achieved."   - William Jennings Bryan

334. "The best and most beautiful things in the world cannot be seen or even touched. They must be felt with the heart." -Helen Keller

335. "We make a living by what we get, we make a life by what we give." -Sir Winston Churchill

336. "The difference between a successful person and others is not a lack of strength, not a lack of knowledge, but rather in a lack of will." -Vince Lombardi

337. "We are what we repeatedly do. Excellence, then, is not an act, but a habit." –Aristotle

338. "Kind words can be short and easy to speak but their echoes are truly endless." -Mother Theresa

339. "Even if you're on the right track, you'll get run over if you just sit there." -Will Rogers

340. "Only those who dare to fail greatly can ever achieve greatly." -Robert Kennedy

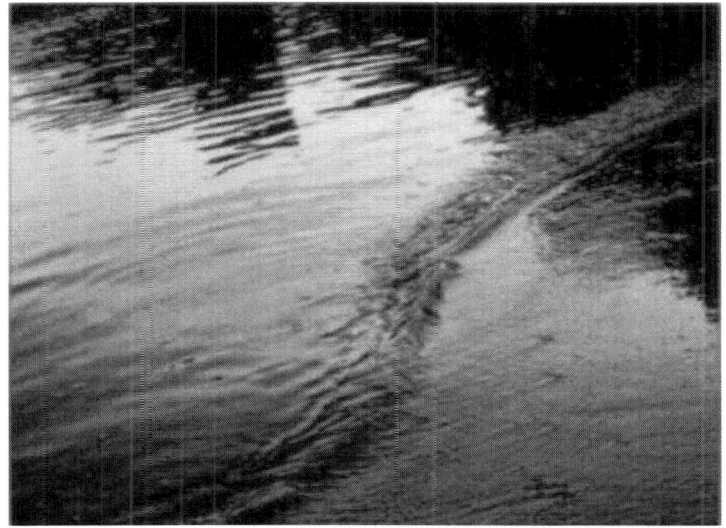

Moyan Brenn/ flickr
http://www.flickr.com/photos/aigle_dore/4179026138/

341. "Nothing great was ever achieved without enthusiasm." -Ralph Waldo Emerson

342. "Small opportunities are often the beginning of great enterprises." –Demosthenes

343. "The ultimate measure of a man is not where he stands in moments of comfort and convenience, but where he stands at times of challenge and controversy." -Martin Luther King, Jr.

344. "Go confidently in the direction of your dreams. Live the life you have imagined." -Henry David Thoreau

345. "If you fail to plan, you plan to fail." -Unknown Author

346. "Keep away from people who belittle your ambitions. Small people always do that, but the really great make you feel that you too can become great." -Mark Twain

347. "Success is to be measured not so much by the position that one has reached in life as by the obstacles which he has overcome while trying to succeed." -Booker T. Washington

348. "The best way to predict the future is to create it." -Peter F. Drucker

349. "You are never given a wish without also being given the power to make it true. You may have work for it, however." -Richard Bach

350. "It's kind of fun to do the impossible." -Walt Disney

351. "The best way to predict the future is to create it." -Peter F. Drucker

352. "Do not let what you cannot do interfere with what you can do." -John Wooden

353. "Pain is inevitable suffering is optional." -Author Unknown

354. "Courage is the price that life exacts for granting peace." -Amelia Earhart

355. "Many of life's failures are people who did not realize how close they were to success when they gave up." -Thomas Edison

356. "Things may come to those who wait, but only the things left by those who hustle." -Abraham Lincoln

357. "To accomplish great things, we must only act, but also dream; not only plan, but also believe." -Anatole France

358. "The most wasted of all days is one without laughter." -E.E Cummings

359. "Give the world the best you have and it may never be enough. Give the world your best anyway." -Mother Teresa

360. "You cannot teach a man anything; you can only help him find it within himself." -Galileo Galilei

361. "You become what you think about." -Earl Nightingale

362. "People will forget what you said, people will forget what you did, but people will never forget how you made them feel." -Maya Angelou

363. "Love cures people – both the ones who give it and the ones who receive it." - Karl A. Menninger

364. "Procrastination is the thief of time." -Edward Young

365. "Too often we underestimate the power of a touch, a smile, a kind word, a listening ear, an honest compliment, or the smallest act of caring, all of which have the potential to turn a life around." -Leo Buscaglia

366. "Everyone thinks of changing the world, but no one thinks of changing himself." -Leo Tolstoy

367. "Opportunities multiply as they are seized." -Sun Tza

368. "Vision without action is a daydream. Action without vision is a nightmare." -Japanese Proverb

369. "The most important thing a father can do for his children is to love their mother." -Unknown Author

370. "Nothing can stop the man with the right mental attitude from achieving his goal; nothing on earth can help the man with the wrong mental attitude." -Thomas Jefferson

Ursula Bach/flickr
http://www.flickr.com/photos/41759352@N05/5703316938/in/photolist-

371. "Tough times never last but tough people do." -Robert Schuller

372. "The best way to cheer yourself up is to try to cheer somebody else up." -Mark Twain

373. "The greatest mistake you can make in life continually fears that you'll make one." -Elbert Hubbard

374. "You can make more friends in two months by becoming interested in other people than you can in two years trying to get other people interested in you." -Dale Carnegie

375. "The mind has exactly the same power as the hands; not merely to grasp the world, but to change it." -Colin Wilson

376. "You can have everything in life you want if you'll just help enough other people get what they want." -Zig Ziglar

377. "How we spend our days is of course how we spend our lives." -Annie Dillard

378. "Your attitude determines your altitude." -Zig Ziglar

379. "It's not whether you get knocked down; it's whether you get back up." -Vinci Lombardi

380. "Change is the law of life. And those who look only to the past or the present are certain to miss the future." -John F. Kennedy

381. "In matters of style, swim with the current; in matters of principle stand like a rock." -Thomas Jefferson

382. "To live a creative life we must lose our fear of being wrong." -Joseph Chilton Pearce

383. "The harder you work, the harder it is to surrender." -Vince Lombardi

384. "It's never too late to be what you might have been." -George Eliot

385. "The man who has no imagination has no wings." -Muhamed Ali

386. "Love like you've never been hurt, dance like no one is watching, live as though heaven is on earth." -Satchel Paige

387. "The greater the obstacle the more glory." –Moliere

388. "I like the dream of the future than the history of the past." -Thomas Jefferson

389. "Opportunities are usually disguised as hard work, so most people don't recognize them." -Ann Landers

390. "Get busy living or get busy dying." -Stephen King

391. "You will do foolish things, but do them with enthusiasm." —Colette

392. "Cherish your visions and your dreams as they are the children of you're the blueprints of your ultimate achievements." -Napoleon Hill

393. "Happiness is when what you think, what you say, and what you do are in harmony." -Mahatma Ghandi

394. "Example is not the main thing in influencing others. It is the only thing.." -Albert Schweitzer

395. "It's never too late to be what you might have been." -George Eliot

396. "Hope springs eternal." -Alexander Pope

397. "The future belongs to those who believe in the beauty of their dreams." -Eleanor Roosevelt

398. "No one can make you feel inferior without your consent." -Eleanor Roosevelt

399. "There are only two ways to live your life. Ones is as though nothing is a miracle. The other is as if everything is." -Albert Einstein

400. "Life is either a daring adventure or nothing at all." -Helen Keller

401. "Far away there in the sunshine are my highest aspirations. I mat not reach them, but I can look up and see their beauty, believe in them, and try to follow where they lead." -Louisa May Alcott

402. "A journey of a thousand miles begins with a single step." —Confucious

403. "You gain strength, courage, and confidence by every experience in which you really stop to look fear in the face." -Eleanor Roosevelt

404. "There is no substitute for hard work." -Thomas Edison

405. "Yesterday is history, tomorrow is a mystery. Today is a gift. That is why it is called the Present." -Author Unknown

406. "Faith can move mountains." -Origin Unknown

407. "Shoot for the moon, Even if you miss, you'll land among the stars." -Les Brown

408. "Don't lose hope; when the sun goes down, the stars come out." -Author Unknown

409. "If you have built castles in the air, your work need not to be lost; that is where they should be. Now put foundations under them." -Henry David Thoreau

410. "Great works are performed not by strength but by perseverance." -Samuel Johnson

411. "Do not wish to be anything but what you are, and try to be that perfectly." -St Francis of De Sales

412. "Men occasionally stumble over the truth, but most of them pick themselves up and hurry off as nothing had happened." -Winston Churchill

413. "Try not to become a man of success but rather try to become a man of value " -Albert Einstein

414. "Happiness is a state of mind." -Author Unknown

415. "Never tell people how to do things. Tell them what to do and they will surprise you with their ingenuity." -General George S. Patton

416. "The difference between the impossible and the possible lies in the person's determination." -Tommy Lasorda

417. "The mind is not a vessel but a fire to be kindled." —Plutarch

418. "A pessimist sees the difficulty in every opportunity; an optimist sees the opportunity in every difficulty." -Sir Winston Churchill

419. "Argue for your limitations. and sure enough they're yours." -Richard Bach

420. "It's always darkest before the dawn." -Author Unknown

421. "The highest reward for a person's toil is not what they get for it, but what they become by it." -John Ruskin

422. "The best relationship is one in which your love for each other exceeds your need for each other." -Author Unknown

423. "Love does not consist in gazing at each other but in looking each other but in looking outward together in the same direction." -Antoine de Saint-Exupery

424. "Happiness lies in the joy of achievement and the thrill of creative effort." -Franklin D. Roosevelt

425. "You have to expect things of yourself before you can do them." -Michael Jordan

426. "The only way to discover the limits of the possible is to go beyond them into the impossible." -Arthur C. Clarke

427. "Watch your thoughts become words, Watch your words; they become actions. Watch your actions; they become habits. Watch your habits; they become character, Watch your character; it becomes your destiny." -Frank Outlaw

428. "You will become as small as your controlling desire; as great as your dominant aspiration." -James Allen

429. "The unexamined life is not worth living." –Socrates

430. "Life isn't about finding yourself. Life is about creating yourself." -George Bernard Shaw

431. "Many receive advise, only the wise profit from it." -Publilius Syrus

432. "It is not the strongest of the species that survive, nor the most intelligent, but the most responsive to change." -Charles Darwin

433. "To succeed..you need to find something to hold on to, something to motivate you, something to inspire you." -Tony Dorsett

434. "When there's life, there's hole." –Terence

435. "The harder I work, the luckier I get." -Samuel Goldwys

436. "The universe is full of magical things patiently waiting for our wits to grow sharper." -Eden Phillpotts

437. "Well done is better than well said." -Benjamin Franklin

438. "When you come to the edge of all the light you know and are about to slep off into the darkness of the unknown, faith is knowing one of two things will happen; There will be something solid to stand on or you will be taught to fly." -Barbara Winter

439. "It is not enough to have a good mind; the main thing is to use it well." -Rene Descartes

440. "Good judgment comes from experience. Experience comes from bad judgment." -Jim Horning

441. "When its dark enough you can see the stars." -Charles A. Beard

442. "Happiness is not a destination. It is a method of life." -Burton Hills

443. "The only good luck many great men ever had was being born with the ability and determination to overcome bad luck." -Channing Pollock

444. "Our life is what are thought make it." -Marcus Aurelius

445. "The definition of insanity is doing the same thing over and over and expecting different results." -Albert Einstein

446. "What would you attempt to do if you knew you could not fail?" -Robert Schuller

447. "Life is a great big canvass and you should throw all the paint you can on it." -Danny Kaye

448. "Better to light the candle than curse the darkness." -Eleanor Roosevelt

449. "Happiness is not something you postpone for the future; it is something you design for the present." -Jim Rohn

450. "God always gives His best to those who leave the choice with him." -Jim Elliot

451. "Your present circumstances don't determine where you can go; they merely determine where you start." -Nido Qubien

452. "If you accept the expectations of others, especially negative ones, then you never will change the outcome." -Michael Jordan

453. "I can't change the direction of the wind, but I can adjust my sails to always reach my destination." -Jimmy Dean

454. "Put your heart, mind, and soul into even your smallest acts. This is the secret of success." -Swami Sivananda

455. "If it were not for hopes, the heart would break." -Thomas Fuller

456. "Wonder rather than doubt is the root of all knowledge." -Abraham Joshua Heschel

457. "Don't limit yourself. Many people limit themselves to what they think they can do. You can go as far as your mind lets you. What you believe, remember, you can achieve." -Mary Kay Ash

458. "It is by acts and not by ideas that people live." -Harry Emerson Fosdick

459. "The power of imagination makes us infinite." -John Muir

460. "Nurture your minds with great thoughts. To believe in the heroic makes heroes." -Benjamin Disraeli

461. "I believe there's an inner power that makes winners or losers. And the winners are the ones who really listen to the truth of their hearts." -Sylvester Stallone

462. "Everyone here has the sense that right now is one of those moments when we are influencing the future." -Steve Jobs

463. "Noble deeds that are concealed are most esteemed." -Blaise Pascal

464. "Space is an inspirational concept that allows you to dream big." -Peter Diamandis

465. "The more difficulties one has encounter, within and without, the more significant and the higher in inspiration his life will be." -Horace Bushnell

466. "Don't wait for extraordinary oppurtunities. Seize common occasions and make them great." -Orison Swett Marden

467. "The power of imagination makes us infinite." -John Muir

468. "Challenges are what make life interesting and overcoming them is what makes life meaningful." -Joshua J. Marine
469. "In order to succeed, your desire for success should be greater than your fear of failure." -Bill Cosby
470. "The only way to do great work is to love what you do. If you haven't found it yet, keep looking. Don't settle." - Steve Jobs
471. "Don't worry about failures, worry about the chances you miss when you don't even try." - Jack Canfield
472. "The only thing that stands between you and your dream is the will to try and the belief that it is actually possible." -Joel Brow
473. "Accept responsibility for your life. Know that it is you who will get you where you want to go, no one else." - Les Brown
474. "It's hard to wait around for something you know might never happen; but its harder to give up when you know its everything you want." -Author Unknown
475. "Happiness cannot be traveled to, owned, earned, or worn. It is the spiritual experience of living every minute with love, grace and gratitude." -Denis Waitley
476. "Don't be afraid to stand for what you believe in, even if that means standing alone. "-Author Unknown
477. "Though no one can go back and make a brand new start, anyone can start from now and make a brand new ending." -Carl Bard
478. "Walk away from anything or anyone who takes away from your joy. Life is too short to put up with fools." -Author Unknown
479. "It is the mark of an educated mind to be able to entertain a thought without accepting it." -Aristotle

480. "Be not afraid of greatness. Some are born great, some achieve greatness, and some have greatness thrust upon 'em." -William Shakespeare

481. "Failure is the condiment that gives success its flavor." -Truman Capote

482. "In between goals is a thing called life that has to be lived and enjoyed." -Sid Caesar

483. "Don't go through life, grow through life." -Eric Butterworth

484. "An obstacle is often a stepping stone." —Prescott

Ursula Bach/flickr
http://www.flickr.com/photos/41759352@N05/5703316938/in/photolist-

485. "Perfection is not attainable, but if we chase perfection we can catch excellence. "-Vince Lombardi

486. "Be more concerned with your character than with your reputation. Your character is what you really are while your reputation is merely what others think you are." -Dale Carnegie

487. "The elevator of success is out of order. You'll have to use the stairs… one step at a time." -Joe Girard

488. "The man who removes a mountain begins by carrying away small stones." -Chinese Proverb

489. "Great spirits have always encountered violent opposition from mediocre minds." -Albert Einstein

490. "Keep on going and the chances are you will stumble on something, perhaps when you are least expecting it. I have never heard of anyone stumbling on something sitting down." -Charles F. Kettering

491. "Do one thing every day that scares you. " - Eleanor Roosevelt

492. "When we love, we always strive to become better than we are. When we strive to become better than we are, everything around us becomes better too."
- Paulo Coelho

493. "The flower that blooms in adversity is the rarest and most beautiful of all."
- Walt Disney Company

Bahman Farzad/flickr
http://www.flickr.com/photos/21644167@N04/5089674479/in/photolist-

494. "It's not the load that breaks you down, it's the way you carry it." - Lou Holtz

495. "What you do makes a difference, and you have to decide what kind of difference you want to make." - Jane Goodall

496. "The things you do for yourself are gone when you are gone, but the things you do for others remain as your legacy." - Kalu Ndukwe Kalu

497. "If you treat an individual as he is, he will remain how he is. But if you treat him as if he were what he ought to be and could be, he will become what he ought to be and could be." - Johann Wolfgang von Goethe

498. "You need to learn how to select your thoughts just the same way you select your clothes every day. This is a power you can cultivate. If you want to control things in your life so bad, work on the mind. That's the only thing you should be trying to control." - Elizabeth Gilbert

499. "One must maintain a little bittle of summer, even in the middle of winter." - Henry David Thoreau

500. "You'll never get ahead of anyone as long as you try to get even with him." - Lou Holtz

501. "The price of greatness is responsibility." - Winston Churchill

502. "It's not what you say out of your mouth that determines your life, it's what you whisper to yourself that has the most power!" - Robert T. Kiyosaki

503. "Obscurity and a competence—that is the life that is best worth living." - Mark Twain

504. "What the superior man seeks is in himself; what the small man seeks is in others." – Confucius

505. "People take different roads seeking fulfillment and happiness. Just because they're not on your road doesn't mean they've gotten lost." - Dalai Lama XIV

506. "You're better than this. Better than whatever it is you're going to do now." - Richelle Mead

507. "For every moment of triumph, for every instance of beauty, many souls must be trampled." - Hunter S. Thompson

508. "Whining is not only graceless, but it can be dangerous. It can alert a brute that a victim is in the neighborhood." - Maya Angelou

509. "The firmest friendships have been formed in mutual adversity,
as iron is most strongly united by the fiercest flame." - Charles Caleb Colton

510. "Reminds us that greatness lies even in the smallest of moments, in the humblest of hearts, and we shall, each of us, be called to greatness. Whether we shall rise to meet it or let it slip away is the challenge put before us all." - Libba Bray

511. "It doesn't matter what you did or where you were...it matters where you are and what you're doing. Get out there! Sing the song in your heart and NEVER let anyone shut you up!!"
- Steve Maraboli

512. "When you look for a man- what you want to look for is a man with the heart of a poor boy and the mind of a conqueror." - C. JoyBell C.

513. "You must not ever stop being whimsical. And you must not, ever, give anyone else the responsibility for your life." - Mary Oliver

514. "Sometimes good things fall apart, so better things can fall together." - Jessica Howell

515. "The person who tries to live alone will not succeed as a human being. His heart withers if it does not answer another heart. His mind shrinks away if he hears only the echoes of his own thoughts and finds no other inspiration. " - Pearl S. Buck

516. "Few people know how to take a walk. The qualifications are endurance, plain clothes, old shoes, an eye for nature, good humor, vast curiosity, good speech, good silence and nothing too much." - Ralph Waldo Emerson

517. "Fear is inevitable, I have to accept that, but I cannot allow it to paralyze me." - Isabel Allende

518. "The laughter of the world is merely loneliness pathetically trying to reassure itself."
- Neal A. Maxwell

519. "If you can't fight and you can't flee, flow." - Robert Elias

520. "Our wounds are often the openings into the best and most beautiful part of us." - David Richo

521. "There's nothing more inspiring than the complexity and beauty of the human heart."   - Cynthia Hand

522. "You are the master of your destiny. You can influence, direct and control your own environment You can make your life what you want it to be." - Napoleon Hill

523. "You cannot expect victory and plan for defeat." - Joel Osteen

524. "Reach high, for stars lie hidden in you. Dream deep, for every dream precedes the goal." - Rabindranath Tagore

525. "The quality of a man's life is in direct proportion to his commitment to excellence, regardless of his chosen field of endeavor. " - Vince Lombardi Jr.

526. "There is no such thing as a problem without a gift for you in its hands. You seek problems because you need their gifts."
- Richard Bach

527. "Cry. Forgive. Learn. Move on. Let your tears water the seeds of your future happiness." - Steve Maraboli

528. "Live your truth. Express your love. Share your enthusiasm. Take action towards your dreams. Walk your talk. Dance and sing to your music. Embrace your blessings. Make today worth remembering." - Steve Maraboli

529. "You couldn't erase the past. You couldn't even change it. But sometimes life offered you the opportunity to put it right. " - Ann Brashares

530. "Instead of focusing on how much you can accomplish, focus on how much you can absolutely love what you're doing."
- Leo Babauta

531. "How you react emotionally is a choice in any situation."
- Judith Orloff

532. "Improvement makes strait roads, but the crooked roads without Improvement, are roads of Genius." - William Blake

533. "It may be that you are not yourself luminous, but that you are a conductor of light. Some people without possessing genius have a remarkable power of stimulating it." - Arthur Conan Doyle

534. "Everything you need to know you have learned through your journey. " - Paulo Coelho

535. "Life doesn't require that we be the best, only that we try our best." - H. Jackson Brown Jr.

536. "Unrequited love is the infinite curse of a lonely heart."
― Christina Westover

mozzercork/flickr
http://www.flickr.com/photos/98382796@N00/109582266/in/photolist-

537. "The probability that we may fail in the struggle ought not to deter us from the support of a cause we believe to be just." - Abraham Lincoln

538. "We believe in ordinary acts of bravery, in the courage that drives one person to stand up for another." - Veronica Roth

539. "We have to allow ourselves to be loved by the people who really love us, the people who really matter. Too much of the time, we are blinded by our own pursuits of people to love us, people that don't even matter, while all that time we waste and the people who do love us have to stand on the sidewalk and watch us beg in the streets! It's time to put an end to this. It's time for us to let ourselves be loved." - C. JoyBell C.

540. "You will find that it is necessary to let things go; simply for the reason that they are heavy. So let them go, let go of them. I tie no weights to my ankles." - C. JoyBell C.

541. "One day, in retrospect, the years of struggle will strike you as the most beautiful." - Sigmund Freud

542. "The unhappiest people in this world, are those who care the most about what other people think." - C. JoyBell C.

543. "Thinking something does not make it true. Wanting something does not make it real." - Michelle Hodkin

544. "No one loses anyone, because no one owns anyone. That is the true experience of freedom: having the most important thing in the world without owning it." - Paulo Coelho

545. "One of the most scariest thing in life,is when you come to the realization that the only thing that can save you,is...yourself." - Demi Lovato

546. "Sometimes, we are so attached to our way of life that we turn down wonderful opportunities simply because don't know what to do with it." - Paulo Coelho

547. "There is something beautiful about all scars of whatever nature. A scar means the hurt is over, the wound is closed and healed, done with." - Harry Crews

548. "Faith moves mountains, love transforms hearts." - John Paul Warren

549. "Do not wait to strike till the iron is hot; but make it hot by striking." - William B. Sprague

550. "What you get by achieving your goals is not as important as what you become by achieving your goals." – Goethe

551. "Whatever you do will be insignificant, but it is very important that you do it." - Mahatma Gandhi

552. "Some succeed because they are destined. Some succeed because they are determined." - Author Unknown

553. "A happy person is not a person in a certain set of circumstances, but rather a person with a certain set of attitudes." - Hugh Downs

554. "Age is an issue of mind over matter. If you don't mind, it doesn't matter." - Mark Twain

555. "The surest way not to fail is to determine to succeed." - Richard B. Sheridan

556. "Many great ideas go unexecuted, and many great executioners are without ideas. One without the other is worthless." - Tim Blixseth

557. "Sometimes you just got to give yourself what you wish someone else would give you." - Dr Phil

558. "Motivation is a fire from within. If someone else tries to light that fire under you, chances are it will burn very briefly." - Stephen R. Covey

559. "Being defeated is only a temporary condition; giving up is what makes it permanent." - Marilyn vos Savant

560. "I can't understand why people are frightened by new ideas. I'm frightened by old ones." - John Cage

561. "There are only two rules for being successful. One, figure out exactly what you want to do, and two, do it." -Mario Cuomo

562. "Success is a state of mind. If you want success, start thinking of yourself as a success." - Dr. Joyce Brothers

563. "An idea can turn to dust or magic, depending on the talent that rubs against it." - Bill Bernbach

564. "To avoid criticism do nothing, say nothing, be nothing." - Elbert Hubbard

565. "The art of being wise is the art of knowing what to overlook." - William James

566. "Don't let life discourage you; everyone who got where he is had to begin where he was." - Richard L. Evans

567. "The only people who find what they are looking for in life are the fault finders." - Foster's Law

568. "Defeat is not bitter unless you swallow it." - Joe Clark

569. "People seem not to see that their opinion of the world is also a confession of character." - Ralph Waldo Emerson

570. "The sun shines and warms and lights us and we have no curiosity to know why this is so; but we ask the reason of all evil, of pain, and hunger, and mosquitoes and silly people." - Ralph Waldo Emerson

571. "If you're going through hell, keep going." - Winston Churchill

572. "The secret to life is meaningless unless you discover it yourself." - W. Somerset Maugham

573. "Be humble enough to admit you're not perfect, but determined enough to strive to be perfect." - Babsie Burke

574. "Life is not about all the wrong moves you made, Life is about the one right move that made all the difference." - James Lockhart

575. "The best revenge is massive success." - Frank Sinatra

576. "Motivation alone is not enough.If you have an idiot and you motivate him,now you have a motivated idiot." - Jim Rohn

577. "All our dreams can come true – if we have the courage to pursue them." - Walt Disney

578. "Opportunity is missed by most people because it is dressed in overalls and looks like work." - Thomas Edison

579. "Pleasure in the job puts perfection in the work." – Aristotle

580. "Pleasure in the job puts perfection in the work." – Aristotle

581. "There is one quality which one must possess to win, and that is definiteness of purpose, the knowledge of what one wants, and a burning desire to possess it." -Napoleon Hill

582. "Believe you can and you're halfway there." - Theodore Roosevelt

583. "Do or do not, there is no try." –Yoda

584. "Experience is the best teacher." –Proverb

585. "Necessity is the mother of invention." –Proverb

586. "Nothing that is outside of you can affect you. Nothing outside of you can make you feel sad, angry, weak or disheartened without your permission." -Author unknown

587. "Defeat is not the worst of failures. Not to have tried is the true failure." -George Edward Woodberry

588. "The true measure of a man is not how he behaves in moments of comfort and convenience but how he stands at times of controversy and challenges. " - Martin Luther King Jr.

589. "Difficulties are meant to rouse, not discourage. The human spirit is to grow strong by conflict." -William Ellery Channing

590. "Accept challenges, so that you may feel the exhilaration of victory." -George S. Patton

591. "Fractures well cured make us more strong." -Ralph Waldo Emerson

592. "A gentleman can withstand hardships; it is only the small man who, when submitted to them, is swept off his feet." —Confucius

593. "The gem cannot be polished without friction, nor man be perfected without trials." -Danish Proverb

594. "It is the surmounting of difficulties that make heroes." -Louis Kossuth

595. "Stand up to your obstacles and do something about them. You will find that they haven't half the strength you think they have." -Norman Vincent Peale

596. "History has demonstrated that the most notable winners usually encountered heartbreaking obstacles before they triumphed. They won because they refused to become discouraged by their defeats." -B. C. Forbes

597. "Obstacles don't have to stop you. If you run into a wall, don't turn around and give up. Figure out how to climb it, go through it, or work around it." -Michael Jordan

598. "It may sound strange, but many champions are made champions by setbacks."
-Bob Richards

599. "Victory is always possible for the person who refuses to stop fighting." -Napoleon Hill

600. "Strength does not come from physical capacity. It comes from an indomitable will." -Mahatma Gandhi

601. "The beauty of the soul shines out when a man bears with composure one heavy mischance after another, not because he does not feel them, but because he is a man of high and heroic temper." —Aristotle

602. "I would never have amounted to anything were it not for adversity. I was forced to come up the hard way." -J. C. Penney

603. "You don't develop courage by being happy in your relationships everyday. You develop it by surviving difficult times and challenging adversity." -Barbara De Angelis

604. "You become a champion by fighting one more round. When things are tough, you fight one more round." -James J. Corbett

605. "The greater the difficulty, the more glory in surmounting it. Skillful pilots gain their reputation from storms and tempests." –Epictetus

606. "Don't give up at half time. Concentrate on winning the second half." -Paul "Bear" Bryant

607. "Every person who wins in any undertaking must be willing to cut all sources of retreat. Only by doing so can one be sure of maintaining that state of mind known as a burning desire to win - essential to success." -Napoleon Hill

608. "Every worthwhile accomplishment, big or little, has its stages of drudgery and triumph; a beginning, a struggle and a victory." –Gandhi

609. "Let us not be content to wait and see what will happen, but give us the determination to make the right things happen." -Peter Marshall

610. "If your determination is fixed, I do not counsel you to despair. Few things are impossible to diligence and skill. Great works are performed not by strength, but perseverance." -Samuel Johnson

611. "Those who wish to sing, always find a song." -Swedish Proverb

612. "To him who is determined it remains only to act." -Italian Proverb

613. "The difference between the impossible and the possible lies in a person's determination." -Tommy Lasorda

614. "It is common sense to take a method and try it. If it fails, admit it frankly and try another. But above all, try something." -Franklin D Roosevelt

Just B Photography/flickr
http://www.flickr.com/photos/30947063@N02/4362833750/

615. "The greatest glory in living lies not in never failing, but in rising every time we fail." -Nelson Mandela

616. "We shall draw from the heart of suffering itself the means of inspiration and survival." -Sir Winston Churchill

617. "You may not realize it when it happens, but a kick in the teeth may be the best thing in the world for you." -Walt Disney

618. "Live out your imagination, not your history." -Stephen Covey

619. "The tragedy of life is not that it ends so soon, but we wait so long to begin it." -Author Unknown

620. "I wish you enough rain to appreciate the sun more." -Author Unknown

621. "One can never consent to creep when one feels an impulse to soar." -Author Unknown

622. "Success seems to be largely a matter of hanging on after others have let go." -William Feather

623. "You cannot shake hands with a clenched fist." -Golda Meir

624. "Action may not always bring happiness but there is no happiness without action." -Benjamin Disraeli

625. "Things turn out best for the people who make the best of their way things turn out." -Art Linkletter

626. "The man who has no imagination has no wings." -Muhamed Ali

627. "Problems are only oppurtunities in work clothes." -Henry Kaiser

628. "The only gift is the portion of thyself." -Ralph Waldo Emerson

629. "Success doesn't come to you, you go to it." -Marva Collins

630. "Little strokes fell great oaks." -Benjamin Franklin

631. "We judge ourselves by what we are capable of doing, while others judge us by what we have already done." -Henry Wadsworth Longfellow

632. "If we did all things we would literally capable of doing we would literally astound ourselves." -Thomas Edison

633. "Your pain is the breaking of the shell that encloses your understanding." -Kahlil Gibran

634. "It's not what happens to you; it's what you do about it that makes the difference."-W. Mitchell

635. "If you want to feel rich just count all the things you have that money can't buy." -Author Unknown

636. "The time to repair the roof is when the sun is shining." -John F. Kennedy

637. "I keep my ideals, because inspite of everything. I still believe that people are really good at heart." -Anne Frank

638. "When I hear somebody sigh, Life is hard, I am always tempted to ask, Compared to what?" -Sydney Harris

639. "The true mystery of the world is the visible, not the invisible." -Oscar Wilde

640. "I am a great believer of luck and I find that the harder I work the more I have of it." -Thomas Jefferson

641. "If we don't change, we don't grow. If we don't grow, we aren't really living." -Gail Sheehy

642. "He who asks a question is a fool for five minutes. He who does not a question is a fool forever." –Chinese Proverb

643. "Every man dies. Not every man truly lives." –Braveheart

644. "Nothing is impossible to a willing heart." –John Keywood

645. "Victory belongs to the most persevering." –Napoleon Bonaparte

646. "Great minds have purposes others have wishes." –Washington Irving

647. "The great end of life is not knowledge but action." –Thomas Henry Huxley

648. "The past does not equal the future." –Anthony Robbins

649. "A happy person is not a person in a certain set of circumstances, but rather a person with certain set of attitudes." –Hugh Down

650. "A man can succeed at almost anything for which he has unlimited enthusiasm." –Charles M. Schwab

651. "People rarely succeed unless they have fun in what they are doing." –Dale Carnegie

652. "We have not yet begun to fight."- John Paul Jones

653. "The future belongs to those who prepare for it today." –Malcolm X

654. "The harder you fall the higher you bounce." –Horace

655. "Failure is the only opportunity to begin again more intelligently." –Henry Ford

656. "Success is the sum of small efforts, repeated day in and day out." –Robert Collier

657. "Our aspirations are our possibilities." –Robert Browning

658. "You are today where your thoughts have brought." –James Allen

659. "Treat a man as he is and he will remain as he is. Treat a man as he can and should be and he will become as he can and should be." –Johann Wolfgang von Goethe

660. "Service is the rent we pay for being. It is the very purpose of life, and not something you do in your spare time." –Marion Wright Edelman

661. "Hide not your talents, they for use were made. What's a sundial in a shade?" –Benjamin Franklin

662. "Practice does not make perfect, perfect practice makes perfect." –Vince Lombardi

663. "Make each day your masterpiece". –John Wooden

664. "Manifest plainness, embrace simplicity. Reduce selfishness, have few desires." –Lao Tzu

665. "If you don't design your own life plan, chances are you'll fall into someone else's plan. And guess what they have planned for you? Not much." -Jim Rohn

666. "Our greatest weakness lies in giving up. The most certain way to succeed is always to try just one more time." -Thomas A. Edison

667. "You are never too old to set another goal or to dream a new dream." -C. S. Lewis

668. "I don't believe you have to be better than everybody else. I believe you have to be better than you ever thought you could be." -Ken Venturi

669. "Always do your best. What you plant now, you will harvest later." -Og Mandino

670. "Even if you fall on your face, you're still moving forward." -Victor Kiam

671. "Expect problems and eat them for breakfast." -Alfred A. Montapert

672. "When you fail you learn from the mistakes you made and it motivates you to work even harder." -Natalie Gulbis

673. "The secret of getting ahead is getting started." -Mark Twain

674. "You need to overcome the tug of people against you as you reach for high goals." -George S. Patton

675. "I learned that we can do anything, but we can't do everything... at least not at the same time. So think of your priorities not in terms of what activities you do, but when you do them. Timing is everything." -Dan Millman

676. "Without hard work, nothing grows but weeds." -Gordon B. Hinckley

677. "The wise does at once what the fool does at last." -Baltasar Gracian

678. "The will to succeed is important, but what's more important is the will to prepare." -Bobby Knight

679. "I've found that luck is quite predictable. If you want more luck, take more chances. Be more active Show up more often." -Brian Tracy

680. "I was motivated to be different in part because I was different." -Donna Brazile

681. "The ultimate aim of the ego is not to see something, but to be something."-Muhammad Iqbal

682. "What is called genius is the abundance of life and health." -Henry David Thoreau

683. "The dog that trots about finds a bone." -Golda Meir

684. "The most dangerous leadership myth is that leaders are born — that there is a genetic factor to leadership. This myth asserts that people simply either have certain charismatic qualities or not. That's nonsense; in fact, the opposite is true. Leaders are made rather than born." –WARREN G. BENNIS

685. "Successful and unsuccessful people do not vary greatly in their abilities. They vary in their desires to reach their potential."–JOHN MAXWELL

686. "If you are going to achieve excellence in big things, you develop the habit in little matters. Excellence is not an exception, it is a prevailing attitude."–CHARLES R. SWINDOLL

687. "Along with success comes a reputation for wisdom." –Euripides

688. "They can because they think they can. " –Virgil

689. "Nothing can stop the man with the right mental attitude from achieving his goal; nothing on earth can help the man with the wrong mental attitude. " –Thomas Jefferson

690. " Keep steadily before you the fact that all true success depends at last upon yourself. " –Theodore T. Hunger

691. "We are all motivated by a keen desire for praise, and the better a man is, the more he is inspired to glory. " –Cicero

692. "The thing always happens that you really believe in; and the belief in a thing makes it happen. " –Frank Loyd Wright

693. "The surest way not to fail is to determine to succeed. " –Richard Brinsley Sheridan

694. "A failure is a man who has blundered, but is not able to cash in on the experience. " –Elbert Hubbard

695. "There is only one success--to be able to spend your life in your own way. " –Christopher Morley

696. "Success is sweet: the sweeter if long delayed and attained through manifold struggles and defeats. " –A. Branson Alcott

697. "The secret of success is to know something nobody else knows. " –Aristotle Onassis

698. "The greatest results in life are usually attained by simple means and the exercise of ordinary qualities. " –Owen Feltham

699. "Failures do what is tension relieving, while winners do what is goal achieving." –Dennis Waitley

700. "The difference between a successful person and others is not a lack of strength, not a lack of knowledge, but rather a lack in will." –Vince Lombardi

701. "Everyone has a fair turn to be as great as he pleases." –Jeremy Collier

702. "I cannot give you the formula for success, but I can give you the formula for failure--which is: Try to please everybody." –Herbert Bayard Swope

703. "Success does not consist in never making blunders, but in never making the same one a second time." –Josh Billings

704. "The secret of success in life is for a man to be ready for his opportunity when it comes." -Earl of Beaconsfield

705. "Success is the good fortune that comes from aspiration, desperation, perspiration and inspiration." –Evan Esar

706. "If you wish success in life, make perseverance your bosom friend, experience your wise counselor, caution your elder brother, and hope your guardian genius." –Jospeph Addison

707. "Impatience never commanded success." –Edwin H. Chapin

708. "The talent of success is nothing more than doing what you can do, well." –Henry W. Longfellow

709. "To climb steep hills requires a slow pace at first." –William Shakespeare

710. "Try not to become a man of success but a man of value." –Albert Einstein

711. "The man who makes a success of an important venture never wails for the crowd. He strikes out for himself. It takes nerve, it

takes a great lot of grit; but the man that succeeds has both. Anyone can fail. The public admires the man who has enough confidence in himself to take a chance. These chances are the main things after all. The man who tries to succeed must expect to be criticized. Nothing important was ever done but the greater number consulted previously doubted the possibility. Success is the accomplishment of that which most people think can't be done. " –C. V. White

712. "If at first you don't succeed, try, try again. Then quit. There's no use being a damn fool about it. " –W.C. Fields

713. "Success is the sum of small efforts, repeated day in and day out. "–Robert Collier

714. "You can have everything you want in life, if you just help enough people get what they want in life." - ZigZiglar

715. "If I have the belief that I can do it, I shall surely acquire the capacity to do it even if I may not have it at the beginning." -Gandhi

716. "Pain is temporary. It may last a minute, or an hour, or a day, or a year, but eventually it will subside and something else will take its place. If I quit, however, it lasts forever." - Lance Armstrong

717. "It takes courage to grow up and become who you really are." -E. E. Cummings

718. "Great minds have great purposes, others have wishes. Little minds are tamed and subdued by misfortune; but great minds rise above them." -Washington Irving

719. "I don't know the key to success, but the key to failure is trying to please everybody."- Bill Cosby

720. "The start is what stops most people."- Don Shula

721. "Happiness is not something you postpone for the future; it is something you design for the present."- Jim Rohn

722. "A difficult time can be more readily endured if we retain the conviction that our existence holds a purpose – a cause to pursue, a person to love, a goal to achieve."- John Maxwell

723. "I realized early on that success was tied to not giving up. Most people in this business gave up and went on to other things If you simply didn't give up, you would outlast the people who came in on the bus with you."- Harrison Ford

724. "We all have dreams. But in order to make dreams come into reality, it takes an awful lot of determination, dedication, self-discipline, and effort."- Jesse Owens

725. "To avoid criticism do nothing, say nothing, be nothing."- Elbert Hubbard

726. "Show me a person who doesn't make mistakes and I'll show you a person who doesn't do anything."- Leonard Rubino

727. "Today I will do what others won't, so tomorrow I can accomplish what others can't."- Jerry Rice

728. "Too many people are thinking the grass is greener on the other side of the fence, when they ought to just water the grass they are standing on."- Amar Dave

729. "The content of your character is your choice. Day by day, what you choose, what you think and what you do is who you become."- Heraclitus

730. "Losers live in the past. Winners learn from the past and enjoy working in the present toward the future."- Denis Waitley

731. "Learn to appreciate what you have, before time makes you appreciate what you had." - Unknown

Terence Pang/ flickr
http://www.flickr.com/photos/terencepang/5853320449/

732. "I fear not the man who has practiced 10,000 kicks once, but I fear the man who has practiced one kick 10,000 times."- Bruce Lee

733. "It is during our failures that we discover our true desire for success."- Kevin Ngo

734. "Often the difference between a successful person and a failure is not one has better abilities or ideas, but the courage that one has to bet on one's ideas, to take a calculated risk – and to act."- Maxwell Maltz

735. "The starting point of all achievement is desire. Keep this constantly in mind. Weak desires bring weak results, just as a small fire makes a small amount of heat."- Napoleon Hill

736. "Don't wait for something big to occur. Start where you are, with what you have, and that will always lead you into something greater."- Mary Manin Morrissey

737. "When the world says, 'Give up', Hope whispers, 'Try it one more time.'"- Anonymous

738. "I am grateful for all of my problems. After each one was overcome, I became stronger and more able to meet those that were still to come. I grew in all my difficulties."- James Cash Penney

739. "Don't let life discourage you; everyone who got where he is had to begin where he was."- Richard L. Evans

740. "Inaction breeds doubt and fear. Action breeds confidence and courage. If you want to conquer fear, do not sit home and think about it. Go out and get busy."- Dale Carnegie

741. "Nothing great has ever been achieved except by those who dared to believe that something inside them was superior to circumstances."- Bruce Barton

742. "Most people would rather be certain they're miserable, than risk being happy."- Robert Anthony

743. "The real person you are is revealed in the moments when you're certain no other person is watching. When no one is watching, you are driven by what you expect of yourself."- Ralph S. Marston, Jr.

744. "Hold yourself responsible for a higher standard than anybody else expects of you. Never excuse yourself. Never pity yourself. Be a hard master to yourself – and be lenient to everybody else."- Henry Ward Beecher

745. "Accept responsibility for your life. Know that it is you who will get you where you want to go, no one else."- Les Brown

746. "You can't just sit and wait for people to give you that golden dream. You've got to get out there and make it happen for yourself."- Diana Ross

747. "Your work is going to fill a large part of your life, and the only way to be truly satisfied is to do what you believe is great work. And the only way to do great work is to love what you do. If you haven't found it yet, keep looking. Don't settle. As with all

matters of the heart, you'll know when you find it. And, like any great relationship, it just gets better and better as the years roll on. So keep looking until you find it. Don't settle."- Steve Jobs

748. "Do just once what others say you can't do, and you will never pay attention to their limitations again."- James R. Cook

749. "One of the most tragic things I know about human nature is that all of us tend to put off living. We are all dreaming of some magical rose garden over the horizon instead of enjoying the roses blooming outside our windows today."- Dale Carnegie

750. "You must constantly ask yourself these questions: Who am I around? What are they doing to me? What have they got me reading? What have they got me saying? Where do they have me going? What do they have me thinking? And most important, what do they have me becoming? Then ask yourself the big question: Is that okay? Your life does not get better by chance, it gets better by change."- Jim Rohn

751. "Your time is limited, so don't waste it living someone else's life. Don't be trapped by dogma — which is living with the results of other people's thinking. Don't let the noise of others' opinions drown out your own inner voice. And most important, have the courage to follow your heart and intuition. They somehow already know what you truly want to become. Everything else is secondary."- Steve Jobs

752. "We have no choice of what color we're born or who our parents are or whether we're rich or poor. What we do have is some choice over what we make of our lives once we're here."- Mildred Taylor

753. "Make sure that your actions and behaviors live up to and reflect the words and ideas, promises and commitments that come out of your mouth."- Steve Farber

754. "History has demonstrated that the most notable winners usually encountered heartbreaking obstacles before they

triumphed. They won because they refused to become discouraged by their defeats."- Bertie Charles Forbes

755. "Keep away from people who try to belittle your ambitions. Small people always do that, but the really great make you feel that you, too, can become great."- Mark Twain

756. "The attitude you have as a parent is what your kids will learn from more than what you tell them. They don't remember what you try to teach them. They remember what you are."- Jim Henson

757. "It isn't what you have, or who you are, or where you are, or what you are doing that makes you happy or unhappy. It is what you think about."- Dale Carnegie

758. "Every great dream begins with a dreamer. Always remember, you have within you the strength, the patience and the passion to reach for the stars to change the world."- Harriet Tubman

759. "All who have accomplished great things have had a great aim, have fixed their gaze on a goal which was high, one which sometimes seemed impossible."- Orison SwettMarden

760. "Each day is a new life. Seize it. Live it."- David Guy Powers

761. "To accomplish great things we must not only act, but also dream, not only plan, but also believe."- Anatole France

762. "Life is what we make it, always has been, always will be."- Grandma Moses

763. "Few people take objectives really seriously. They put average effort into too many things, rather than superior thought and effort into a few important things. People who achieve the most are selective as well as determined."- Richard Koch

764. "You must take personal responsibility. You cannot change the circumstances, the seasons, or the wind, but you can change yourself."- Jim Rohn

Moyan Brenn/flickr
http://www.flickr.com/photos/aigle_dore/4103331038/

765. "You never know how strong you are until being strong is the only choice you have."- Unknown

766. "The happiness of your life depends upon the quality of your thoughts."- Marcus Aurelius

767. "Life's challenges are not supposed to paralyze you, they're supposed to help you discover who you are."- Bernice Johnson Reagon

768. "Things work out best for those who make the best of how things work out."- John Wooden

769. "It is not what they take away from you that counts. It's what you do with what you have left."- Hubert Humphrey

770. "You may never know what results come from your action. But if you do nothing, there will be no result."- Gandhi

771. "Remember you will not always win. Some days, the most resourceful individual will taste defeat. But there is, in this case, always tomorrow – after you have done your best to achieve success today."- Maxwell Maltz

772. "The greatest mistake you can make in life is to be continually fearing you will make one."- Elbert Hubbard

773. "Let us not be content to wait and see what will happen, but give us the determination to make the right things happen."- Horace Mann

774. "If you limit your choices only to what seems possible or reasonable, you disconnect yourself from what you truly want, and all that is left is a compromise."- Robert Fritz

775. "It is under the greatest adversity that there exists the greatest potential for doing good, both for oneself and others."- Dalai Lama

776. "I do it because I can; I can because I want to; I want to because you said I couldn't."- Unknown

777. "A journey of a thousand miles begins with a single step."- Lao Tzu

778. "The future belongs to those who believe in the beauty of their dreams."- Eleanor Roosevelt

779. "In the end, what we regret most are the chances we never took."- Frasier Krane

780. "Never give up on what you really want to do. The person with big dreams is more powerful than one with all the facts."- Unknown

781. "You were not born a winner, and you were not born a loser. You are what you make yourself to be."- Lou Holtz

782. "Things don't go wrong and break your heart so you can become bitter and give up. They happen to break you down

and build you up so you can be all that you were intended to be."- Charlie Jones

783. "People who say it cannot be done should not interrupt those who are doing it."- Unknown

784. "Courage doesn't always roar. Sometimes courage is the quiet voice at the end of the day saying, 'I will try again tomorrow.'"- Mary Anne Radmacher

785. "If you argue for your limitations, sure enough, they're yours."- Richard Bach

786. "Every time you stay out late; every time you sleep in; every time you miss a workout; every time you don't give 100%... you make it that much easier for me to beat you."- Unknown

787. "One of the most common causes of failure is the habit of quitting when one is overtaken by temporary defeat."- Napoleon Hill

788. "Believe in possibilities. Believe in human potential. Believe in yourself and you'll have the power to change your fate."- Kevin Ngo

789. "It is during our failures that we discover our true desire for success." - Kevin Ngo

790. "Never continue in a job you don't enjoy. If you're happy in what you're doing, you'll like yourself, you'll have inner peace. And if you have that, along with physical health, you will have had more success than you could possibly have imagined."- Johnny Carson

791. "Success is the sum of small efforts repeated day in and day out."- R. Colier

792. "It's not what happens to you that determines how far you will go in life; it is how you handle what happens to you."- ZigZiglar

793. "At least eighty percent of millionaires are self-made. That is, they started with nothing but ambition and energy, the same way most of us start."- Brian Tracy

794. "When you get right down to the root of the meaning of the word "succeed," you find that it simply means to follow through."- F. W. Nichol

795. "People of mediocre ability sometimes achieve outstanding success because they don't know when to quit. Most men succeed because they are determined to."- George E. Allen

796. "When I thought I couldn't go on, I forced myself to keep going My success is based on persistence, not luck."- Estee Lauder

797. "The chief cause of failure and unhappiness is trading what we want most for what we want at the moment."-Unknown

798. "People get what they want in life when they reach the point at which they can see themselves having what they seek."- Thomas D. Willhite

799. "It doesn't matter who you are, where you come from. The ability to triumph begins with you. Always."-Oprah Winfrey

800. "Perseverance is a great element of success. If you only knock long enough at the gate, you are sure to wake up somebody."- Longfellow

801. "The will to win, the desire to succeed, the urge to reach your full potential… these are the keys that will unlock the door to personal excellence."- Eddie Robinson

802. "Happiness lies in the joy of achievement and the thrill of creative effort."- Franklin Roosevelt

803. "The road to success is lined with many tempting parking spaces."- Unknown

804. "Somehow I can't believe that there are any heights that can't be scaled by a man who knows the secrets of making dreams come true. This special secret, it seems to me, can be summarized in four C s. They are curiosity, confidence, courage, and constancy, and the greatest of all is confidence. When you believe in a thing, believe in it all the way, implicitly and unquestionable."-Walt Disney

805. "The greatest crime in the world is not developing your potential. When you do what you do best, you are helping not only yourself, but the world."- Roger Williams

806. "Believe Big. The size of your success is determined by the size of your belief. Think little goals and expect little achievements. Think big goals and win big success. Remember this, too! Big ideas and big plans are often easier -certainly no more difficult – than small ideas and small plans."- David J. Schwartz

807. "When you put a date on your dream, it becomes a goal. When you aim for the goal, it becomes a challenge. When you beat the challenge, the reward is success. To have success… you need a dream…"- Raja Akhtar

808. "There are two kinds of people in the world: those who make excuses and those who get results. An excuse person will find any excuse for why a job was not done, and a results person will find any reason why it can be done. Be a creator, not a reactor."- Alan Cohen

809. "Think success and it will happen….Think failure and it will happen…."- Thomas D. Willhite

810. "Success isn't a result of spontaneous combustion. You must set yourself on fire."-Arnold H. Glasow

811. "If you live just for today, to make today the most successful, happy day of your life, I am sure that you will have an extraordinary life. A successful life is nothing more than a series of successful days."- Unknown

812. "Whatever it is you want you can have, provided:
    (1) You can state specifically what it is.
    (2) You want it so badly that it becomes a consuming desire in your life.
    (3) You have faith in your ability to achieve it.
    (4) You are persistent in your efforts.
    (5) You are willing to pay the price for success, whatever that price may be." -Thomas D. Willhite

813. "You are your greatest asset. Put your time, effort and money into training, grooming, and encouraging your greatest asset."- Tom Hopkins

814. "Always continue the climb. It is possible for you to do whatever you choose, if you first get to know who you are and are willing to work with a power that is greater than ourselves to do it."- Oprah Winfrey

815. "The Constitution only gives people the right to pursue happiness. You have to catch it yourself…"- Benjamin Franklin

816. "The minute you settle for less than you deserve, you get even less than you settled for."- Maureen Dowd

817. "The road to happiness lies in two simple principles; find what interests you and that you can do well, and put your whole soul into it – every bit of energy and ambition and natural ability you have."- John D. Rockefeller

818. "Live with intention. Walk to the edge. Listen hard. Practice wellness. Play with abandon. Laugh. Choose with no regret. Appreciate your friends. Continue to learn. Do what you love. Live as if this is all there is."- Mary Ann Radmacher

819. "There is nothing in a caterpillar that tells you it's going to be a butterfly."- R. Buckminster Fuller

820. "If you are not criticized, you may not be doing much."- Donald H. Rumsfeld

821. "A wise man will make more opportunities than he finds."-Sir Francis Bacon

822. "You're on the road to success when you realize that failure is only a detour."-Unknown

823. "Success usually comes to those who are too busy to be looking for it."- Henry David Thoreau

824. "Success is a state of mind. If you want success, start thinking of yourself as a success."- Joyce Brothers

825. "However beautiful the strategy, you should occasionally look at the results."- Winston Churchill

826. "Winners are losers who got up and gave it one more try."- Dennis DeYoung

827. "Success is not the key to happiness. Happiness is the key to success. If you love what you are doing, you will be successful."- Albert Schweitzer

828. "I do the very best I know how – the very best I can; and mean to keep doing so until the end. If the end brings me out all right, what is said against me won't amount to anything."- Abraham Lincoln

829. "It is good to have money and the things that money can buy, but it's good too, to check up once in a while and make sure you haven't lost the things money can't buy."- George Lorimer

830. "My mother drew a distinction between achievement and success. She said that achievement is the knowledge that you have studied and worked hard and done the best that is within you. Success is being praised by others. That is nice but not as important or satisfying. Always aim for achievement and forget about success."- Helen Hayes

831. "If you want to succeed in the world you must make your own opportunities as you go on. The man who waits for some

seventh wave to toss him on dry land will find that the seventh wave is a long time a-coming. You can commit no greater folly than to sit by the road side until someone comes along and invites you to ride with him to wealth or influence."- John B. Gough

832. "Successful people are always looking for opportunities to help others. Unsuccessful people are always asking, 'What's in it for me?'"- Brian Tracy

833. "You cannot change your destination overnight, but you can change your direction overnight."- Jim Rohn

834. "No one lives long enough to learn everything they need to learn starting from scratch. To be successful, we absolutely, positively have to find people who have already paid the price to learn the things that we need to learn to achieve our goals."- Brian Tracy

835. "It has been my observation that most people get ahead during the time that others waste."- Henry Ford

836. "Success usually comes to those who are too busy to be looking for it."-Henry Thoreau

837. "Love what you do. Believe in your instincts. And you'd better be able to pick yourself up and brush yourself off every day."-Unknown

838. "Success means having the courage, the determination, and the will to become the person you believe you were meant to be."- George Sheehan

839. "Ask yourself what you would do even if you were never paid. That's a clue to what you should be doing and of course finding a way to be paid for it."- Dr. Joe Vitale

840. "Success is getting what you want. Happiness is wanting what you get."- Dale Carnegie

841. "If you live just for today, to make today the most successful, happy day of your life, I am sure that you will have an extraordinary life. A successful life is nothing more than a series of successful days."- Thomas D. Willhite

842. "If you don't go after what you want, you'll never have it. If you don't ask, the answer is always no. If you don't step forward, you're always in the same place."- Nora Roberts

843. "Pain is temporary. It may last a minute, or an hour, or a day, or a year, but eventually it will subside and something else will take its place. If I quit, however, it lasts forever."- Lance Armstrong

844. "Everyone who has ever taken a shower has had an idea. It's the person who gets out of the shower, dries off, and does something about it that makes a difference."- Nolan Bushnell

845. "The money I have is in direct proportion to the value I've given to others. The more I give of myself, incredibly, the more economic power comes my way."- Tod Barnhart

846. "Be careful the environment you choose for it will shape you; be careful the friends you choose for you will become like them."- W. Clement Stone

847. "Every decision you make – every decision – is not a decision about what to do. It's a decision about Who You Are. When you see this, when you understand it, everything changes. 165"You begin to see life in a new way. All events, occurrences, and situations turn into opportunities to do what you came here to do."- Neale Donald Walsch

848. "Success doesn't come to you… you go to it."- Marva Collins

849. "Everything you need you already have. You are complete right now, you are a whole, total person, not an apprentice person on the way to someplace else. Your completeness must be understood by you and experienced in your thoughts as your own personal reality."- Wayne Dyer

850. "Once failure leads to change…change will then lead toward success.- Stefan Rudolph

851. "I believe the best leaders are the ones that are focused on bringing out the best in their people – transforming lives. When someone has that as their purpose, the profits just naturally follow."- Susan Bagyura

852. "Even if you are on the right track, you'll get run over if you just sit there."-Will Rogers

853. "It is better to wear out than to rust out."-Richard Cumberland

854. "Don't let the fear of the time it will take to accomplish something stand in the way of your doing it. The time will pass anyway; we might just as well put that passing time to the best possible use."-Earl Nightingale

855. "Action may not always bring happiness; but there is no happiness without action."-Benjamin Disraeli

856. "Don't waste life in doubts and fears; spend yourself on the work before you, well assured that the right performance of this hour's duties will be the best preparation for the hours and ages that will follow it."-Ralph Waldo Emerson

857. "It's not what happens to you that determines how far you will go in life; it is how you handle what happens to you."-ZigZiglar

858. "At least eighty percent of millionaires are self-made. That is, they started with nothing but ambition and energy, the same way most of us start."-Brian Tracy

859. "When you get right down to the root of the meaning of the word "succeed," you find that it simply means to follow through."-F. W. Nichol

860. "Anyone who has never made a mistake has never tried anything new."-Albert Einstein

861. "The truth is you can acquire any quality you want by acting as though you already have it."-Joseph Murphy

862. "You must get good at one of two things; planting in the spring or begging in the fall."-Jim Rohn

863. "Everything you want is out there waiting for you to ask. Everything you want also wants you. But you have to take action to get it."-Jack Canfield

864. "It is our attitude at the beginning of a difficult task which, more than anything else, will affect its successful outcome."-William James

865. "We all need a daily check up from the neck up to avoid stinkin 'thinkin' which ultimately leads to hardening of the attitudes."-ZigZiglar

866. "You don't have to have a bad attitude to get a better one. All too often we resist a change because we assume change means that we were "not OK" which hurts our self-image."-Thomas D. Willhite

867. "Any person capable of angering you becomes your master; he can anger you only when you permit yourself to be disturbed by him."-Epictetus

868. "Our ultimate freedom is the right and power to decide how anybody or anything outside ourselves will affect us."-Stephen R. Covey

869. "The greatest revolution of our generation is the discovery that human beings, by changing the inner attitudes of their minds, can change the outer aspects of their lives."-William James

870. "Four short words sum up what has lifted most successful individuals above the crowd: a little bit more. They did all that was expected of them and a little bit more."-A. Lou Vickery

871. "If things are not going well with you, begin your effort at correcting the situation by carefully examining the service you are rendering, and especially the spirit in which you are rendering it."-Roger Babson

872. "Building a habit is the process of educating the subconscious. I have said that you are responsible for changing those attitudes you do not like…and that you can do this by changing the attitude (feeling) itself or by changing your behavior." -Thomas D. Willhite

873. "The longer I live, the more I realize the impact of attitude on life.

874. Attitude, to me, is more important than facts. It is more important than the past, than education, than money, than circumstances, than failures, than successes, than what other people think or say or do. It is more important than appearance, giftedness or skill. It will make or break a company… a church… a home.

875. The remarkable thing is we have a choice every day regarding the attitude we will embrace for that day. We cannot change our past… we cannot change the fact that people will act in a certain way. We cannot change the inevitable. The only thing we can do is play on the one string we have, and that is our attitude… I am convinced that life is 10% what happens to me and 90% how I react to it.

876. And so it is with you… we are in charge of our attitudes." -Charles Swincoll

877. "YOU ARE RESPONSIBLE FOR YOU. Assuming a responsibility means changing a wrong into a right. In other words, if the way you feel is not right, then assuming responsibility means changing it."-Thomas D. Willhite

878. "Look at everything as though you were seeing it either for the first or last time. Then your time on earth will be filled with glory."-Betty Smith

879. "To be a great champion you must believe you are the best. If you're not, pretend you are."-Muhammad Ali

880. "If you fix in your mind the idea that your earning ability is limited, then indeed it is. You will never earn more than that self-set limit. The subconscious will create and maintain the limits you set."-Thomas D. Willhite

881. "People get what they want in life when they reach the point at which they can see themselves having what they seek."-Thomas D. Willhite

882. "I think perfectionism is based on the obsessive belief that if you run carefully enough, hitting each stepping-stone just right, you won't have to die. The truth is you will die anyway and that a lot of people who aren't even looking at their feet are going to do a whole lot better than you, and have a lot more fun while they're doing it."-Anne Lamott

883. "Most people don't affect Reality in a consistent substantial way, because they don't believe they can. They write an intention and then they erase it because they think that's silly. I mean, I can't do that. And then they write it again, and then they erase it. So, time average, it's a very small effect. And it really comes down to the fact that they believe they can't do it."-William Tiller, Ph.D.

884. "People who consider themselves victims of their circumstances will always remain victims unless they develop a greater vision for their lives."-Stedman Graham

885. "If you are looking for yourself, believe me, you will never find "you" because you are what you believe you can become. You, and you alone CREATE your own identity."-Thomas D. Willhite

886. "Never say anything about yourself you do not want to come true."-Brian Tracy

887. "The height of your accomplishments will equal the depth of your convictions."-William F. Scolavino

888. "It's not what you look at that matters, it's what you see."-Henry David Thoreau

889. "To accomplish great things, we must not only act, but also dream; not only plan, but also believe."-Anatole France

890. "People get what they want in life when they reach the point at which they can see themselves having what they seek."-Thomas D. Wilhite

891. "Believe Big. The size of your success is determined by the size of your belief. Think little goals and expect little achievements. Think big goals and win big success. Remember this, too! Big ideas and big plans are often easier -certainly no more difficult – than small ideas and small plans."-David J. Schwartz

892. "Too many people overvalue what they are not and undervalue what they are."-Malcolm Forbes

893. "It's a strange thing, you have said it thousands of times I am sure… you will never know what you can do until you try. However the sad truth is, that most people never try anything until they know they can do it."-Bob Proctor

894. "You are always a valuable, worthwhile human being – not because anybody else says so, not because you're making lots of money – but because you decide to know it."-Dr. Wayne W. Dyer

895. "Your chances of success in any undertaking can always be measured by your belief in yourself."-Robert Collier

896. "A belief is not an idea held by the mind, it is an idea that holds the mind."-Elly Roselle

897. "Believe you can and you're halfway there."-Theodore Roosevelt

898. "Man often becomes what he believes himself to be. If I keep on saying to myself that I cannot do a certain thing, it is possible that I may end by really becoming incapable of doing it. On the

contrary, if I have the belief that I can do it, I shall surely acquire the capacity to do it even if I may not have it at the beginning."-Mahatma Gandhi

899. "The Creator has not given you a longing to do that which you have no ability to do."-Orison SwettMarden

900. "Other people's opinion of you does not have to become your reality."-Les Brown

901. "The minute you settle for less than you deserve, you get even less than you settled for."-Maureen Dowd

902. "Nothing splendid has ever been achieved except by those who dared believe that something inside them was superior to circumstance."-Bruce Barton

903. "Only as high as I reach can I grow, only as far as I seek can I go, only as deep as I look can I see, only as much as I dream can I be."-Karen Ravn

904. "We will act consistently with our view of who we truly are, whether that view is accurate or not."-Anthony Robbins

905. "There is nothing in a caterpillar that tells you it's going to be a butterfly."-R. Buckminster Fuller

906. "One of the greatest discoveries a man makes, one of his great surprises, is to find he can do what he was afraid he couldn't do."-Henry Ford

907. "All of us were meant to be happy and successful. Life is more than a two week vacation once a year. It is, and can be, exactly what you want it to be. There are no limits except those you put on yourself."-Thomas D. Willhite

908. "Ability is what you're capable of doing. Motivation determines what you do. Attitude determines how well you do it."-Lou Holtz

909. "Every person is the creation of himself, the image of his own thinking and believing. As individuals think and believe, so they are."-Claude M. Bristol

910. "People become really quite remarkable when they start thinking that they can do things. When they believe in themselves, they have the first secret of success."-Norman Vincent Peale

911. "When you develop yourself to the point where your belief in yourself is so strong that you know you can accomplish anything you put your mind to, your future will be unlimited."-Brian Tracy

912. "Believe in your dreams and they may come true; believe in yourself and they will come true."-Author Unknown

913. "Believe it can be done. When you believe something can be done, really believe, your mind will find the ways to do it. Believing a solution paves the way to solution."-David Joseph Schwartz

914. "Every single life only becomes great when the individual sets upon a goal or goals which they really believe in, which they can really commit themselves to, which they can put their whole heart and soul into."-Brian Tracy

915. "Every time you state what you want or believe, you're the first to hear it. It's a message to both you and others about what you think is possible. Don't put a ceiling on yourself."-Oprah Winfrey

916. "If you believe in what you are doing, then let nothing hold you up in your work. Much of the best work of the world has been done against seeming impossibilities. The thing is to get the work done."-Dale Carnegie

917. "Men often become what they believe themselves to be. If I believe I cannot do something, it makes me incapable of doing it. But when I believe I can, then I acquire the ability to do it even if I didn't have it in the beginning."-Mahatma Gandhi

918. "The future belongs to those who believe in the beauty of their dreams."-Eleanor Roosevelt

919. "The only thing that stands between a man and what he wants from life is often merely the will to try it and the faith to believe that it is possible."-David Viscott

920. "We all have our own life to pursue, our own kind of dream to be weaving. And we all have the power to make wishes come true, as long as we keep believing."-Louisa May Alcott

921. "Whatever you vividly imagine, ardently desire, sincerely believe, and enthusiastically act upon must inevitably come to pass."-Paul J. Meyer

922. "It is a lesson which all history teaches the wise, to put trust in ideas, and not in circumstances"-Ralph Waldo Emerson

923. "The real winners in life are the people who look at every situation with an expectation that they can make it work or make it better."-Barbara Pletcher

924. "The only thing that stands between you and success is the man in the mirror."-Sean Bain

925. "I may not always be perfect, but I'm always me."-Unknown

926. "To succeed in life, you need two things: ignorance and confidence."- Mark Twain

927. "Confidence is contagious. So is lack of confidence."-Vince Lombardi

928. "You gain strength, courage, and confidence by every experience in which you really stop to look fear in the face. You are able to say to yourself, "I lived through this horror. I can take the next thing that comes along.""- Eleanor Roosevelt

929. "Inaction breeds doubt and fear. Action breeds confidence and courage. If you want to conquer fear, do not sit home and think about it. Go out and get busy."- Dale Carnegie

930. "The man who trims himself to suit everybody will soon whittle himself away."- Charles Schwab

931. "Confidence comes not from always being right but from not fearing to be wrong."- Peter T. Mcintyre

932. "Nobody can make you feel inferior without your consent."-Eleanor Roosevelt

933. "Smile, for everyone lacks self-confidence and more than any other one thing a smile reassures them."- Andre Maurois

934. "To wish you were someone else is to waste the person you are."- Unknown

935. "Experience tells you what to do; confidence allows you to do it."- Stan Smith

936. "Confidence is preparation. Everything else is beyond your control."- Richard Kline

937. "To live you have to experiment, to have the ability to experiment you have to have confidence, to have confidence you have to be loved, to be loved you have to love."- Unknown

938. "Confidence is a habit that can be developed by acting as if you already had the confidence you desire to have."- Unknown

939. "The man who has confidence in himself gains the confidence of others."- Hasidic Saying

940. "Believe in yourself! Have faith in your abilities! Without a humble but reasonable confidence in your own powers you cannot be successful or happy."- Norman Vincent Peale

941. "If I have lost confidence in myself, I have the universe against me."- Ralph Waldo Emerson

942. "The best way to gain self-confidence is to do what you are afraid to do."- Unknown

943. "Whether you think you can or think you can't you are right."- Henry Ford

944. "Confidence comes from hours and days and weeks and years of constant work and dedication."- Roger Staubach

945. "As soon as you trust yourself, you will know how to live."- Johann von Goethe

946. "Never bend your head. Hold it high. Look the world straight in the eye."- Helen Keller

947. "The man who cannot believe in himself cannot believe in anything else."- Roy L. Smith

948. "Search and you will find that at the base and birth of every great business organization was an enthusiast, a man consumed with earnestness of purpose, with confidence in his powers, with faith in the worthwhileness of his endeavors."- Bertie Charles Forbes

949. "A hero is no braver than an ordinary man, but he is braver five minutes longer."-Ralph Waldo Emerson

950. "I think perfectionism is based on the obsessive belief that if you run carefully enough, hitting each stepping-stone just right, you won't have to die. The truth is you will die anyway and that a lot of people who aren't even looking at their feet are going to do a whole lot better than you, and have a lot more fun while they're doing it."-Anne Lamott

951. "Life begins at the end of your comfort zone."-Neale Donald Walsch

952. "Avoiding danger is no safer in the long run than outright exposure. The fearful are caught as often as the bold."-Helen Keller

953. "I am an old man and have known a great many troubles, but most of them never happened."-Mark Twain

954. "Success is not measured by what you accomplish but by the opposition you have encountered, and the courage with which you have maintained the struggle against overwhelming odds."-Orison SwettMarden

955. "It is better by noble boldness to run the risk of being subject to half the evils we anticipate than to remain in cowardly listlessness for fear of what might happen."-Herodotus

956. "Daring ideas are like chessmen moved forward; they may be beaten, but they may start a winning game."-Johann Wolfgang von Goethe

957. "Accept the challenges, so you may feel the exhilaration of victory."-George S. Patton

958. "Far better it is to dare mighty things, to win glorious triumphs, even though checkered by failure, than to take rank with those poor souls who neither enjoy much nor suffer much, because they live in the gray twilight that knows neither victory nor defeat."-Theodore Roosevelt

959. "Somehow I can't believe that there are any heights that can't be scaled by a man who knows the secrets of making dreams come true. This special secret, it seems to me, can be summarized in four C s. They are curiosity, confidence, courage, and constancy, and the greatest of all is confidence. When you believe in a thing, believe in it all the way, implicitly and unquestionable."-Walt Disney

960. "Become so wrapped up in something that you forget to be afraid."-Lady Bird Johnson

961. "Imaginary obstacles are insurmountable. Real ones aren't. But you can't tell the difference when you have no real information. Fear can create even more imaginary obstacles than ignorance can. That's why the smallest step away from speculation and into reality can be an amazing relief…The Reality Solution means: Do it before you're ready."-Barbara Sher

962. "Courage is not the absence of fear, but rather the judgment that something else is more important than fear."-Ambrose Redmoon

963. "All our dreams can come true, if we have the courage to pursue them."-Walt Disney

964. "The lust for comfort, that stealthy thing that enters the house as a guest, and then becomes a host, and then a master."-Kahlil Gibran

965. "The difference between getting somewhere and nowhere is the courage to make an early start. The fellow who sits still and does just what he is told will never be told to do big things."-Charles M. Schwab

966. "Courage is resistance to fear, mastery of fear — not absence of fear."-Mark Twain

967. "Courage doesn't always roar. Sometimes courage is the quiet voice at the end of the day, saying, 'I will try again tomorrow.'"-Mary Anne Radmacher

968. "Courage is the power to let go of the familiar."-Raymond Lindquist

969. "You've got to follow your passion. You've got to figure out what it is you love—who you really are. And have the courage to do that. I believe that the only courage anybody ever needs is the courage to follow your own dreams."-Oprah Winfrey

970. "Take risks: If you win, you will be happy; if you lose, you will be wise."-Anonymous

971. "You gain strength, courage, and confidence by every experience in which you really stop to look fear in the face. You are able to say to yourself, "I have lived through this horror. I can take the next thing that comes along." . . . You must do the thing you think you cannot do. "-Eleanor Roosevelt

972. "It is not the critic who counts, nor the man who points out how the strong man stumbled, or where the doer of deeds could have done them better. The credit belongs to the man who is actually in the arena, whose face is marred by dust and sweat and blood; who strives valiantly; who errs and comes short again and again; who knows great enthusiasms, great devotions; who spends himself in a worthy cause; who, at the best, knows in the end the triumph of high achievement, and who, at the worst, if he fails, at least fails while daring greatly, so that his place shall never be with those timid souls who know neither victory nor defeat "-Theodore Roosevelt

973. "With courage you will dare to take risks, have the strength to be compassionate, and the wisdom to be humble. Courage is the foundation of integrity."-Keshavan Nair

974. "The person who gets the farthest is generally the one who is willing to do and dare. The sure-thing boat never gets far from shore."-Dale Carnegie

975. "He who is afraid to ask is ashamed of learning."-Danish Proverb

976. "People who ask confidently get more than those who are hesitant and uncertain. When you've figured out what you want to ask for, do it with certainty, boldness and confidence."-Jack Canfield

977. "Freedom is not worth having if it does not include the freedom to make mistakes."-Mahatma Gandhi

978. "Courage doesn't always roar. Sometimes courage is the quiet voice at the end of the day saying, "I will try again tomorrow."-Mary Anne Radmacher

979. "Only those who will risk going too far can possibly find out how far one can go."-T.S. Eliot

980. "Far better it is to dare mighty things, to win glorious triumphs, even though checkered by failure, than to take rank with those poor spirits who neither enjoy much nor suffer much, because they live in the gray twilight that knows not victory nor defeat."-Theodore Roosevelt

981. "Unless you try to do something beyond what you have already mastered, you will never grow."-Ralph Waldo Emerson

982. "If you have the courage to begin, you have the courage to succeed."-David Viscott

983. "What keeps so many people back is simply unwillingness to pay the price, to make the exertion, the effort to sacrifice their ease and comfort. " -Orison SwettMardenDecision

984. "A person can make a decision in three ways: positively, negatively, or a decision not to make a decision. In all cases, a person is responsible for, and reaps the benefits or problems associated with that decision." -Thomas D. Willhite

985. "Things which matter most must never be at the mercy of things which matter least." -Johann Von Goethe

986. "We can choose how we want to feel, by choosing how we behave. WE FEEL THE WAY WE BEHAVE. So if you don't like the way you feel, then change your behavior." -Thomas D. Willhite

987. "The chief cause of failure and unhappiness is trading what we want most for what we want at the moment." –unknown

988. "Are you one of the few who writes his own destiny? I hope so. I hope you will have the joy and thrill of waking up to a day you create the way you choose to create it. To me this is happiness: not wealth nor power nor fame but, instead, the

inner strength to say, "I did it my way…and am glad for it." -Thomas D. Willhite

989. "How true Daddy's words were when he said: all children must look after their own upbringing. Parents can only give good advice or put them on the right paths, but the final forming of a person's character lies in their own hands." -Anne Frank

990. "Stop looking at life through a keyhole…open the door to opportunity… get involved, and CREATE the YOU that you CHOOSE to become." -Thomas D. Willhite

991. "The indispensable first step to getting the things you want out of life is this: decide what you want." -Ben Stein

992. "Our ultimate freedom is the right and power to decide how anybody or anything outside ourselves will affect us." -Stephen R. Covey

993. "Every choice you make has an end result." –Zig Ziglar

994. "If you are looking for yourself, believe me, you will never find "you" because you are what you believe you can become. You, and you alone CREATE your own identity." -Thomas D. Willhite

995. "If you were granted one wish, and only one, what would it be? Of all things…wealth, power, wisdom, love, liberty…what would you choose? This may seem fanciful; not so, IT IS REALITY. What you choose to think about, to concentrate on with all your mental power, will, indeed, become a reality. So choose carefully." -Thomas D. Willhite

996. "You've got a lot of choices. If getting out of bed in the morning is a chore and you're not smiling on a regular basis, try another choice." -Steven D. Woodhull

997. "If you want happiness, create it now. Find the joy and beauty of this moment. Give yourself permission to be happy now. Give yourself permission to be beautiful now. Decide at this

moment to be a leader, and you have become one. It can be that fast. "Taking responsibility" is not difficult. It is the "deciding to take responsibility" that is hard." -Thomas D. Willhite

998. "Now is the time. Needs are great, but your possibilities are greater."-Bill Blackman

999. "An optimist expects his dreams to come true; a pessimist expects his nightmares to."-Laurence J. Peter

1000. "The power of imagination makes us infinite."-John Muir

Printed in Germany
by Amazon Distribution
GmbH, Leipzig